HAPPINESS HABITAT

Optimize Your Opportunity Zone

Jacqlyn Burnett

Copyright © 2023 by **Jacqlyn Burnett** — All rights reserved

No part of this book may be reproduced or transmitted in any form or by any means; electronic or mechanical, including photocopying, recording, or by an information storage and retrieval system without permission in writing from the author.

HAPPINESS HABITAT

Print Book ISBN: 979-8-218-21915-4

E-Book ISBN: 979-8-9886230-0-7

Cover design: Jacqlyn Burnett

"You're an asset to the planet."

— Mark Burnett

TABLE OF CONTENTS

FOREWORD by David Meltzer -- 7

PREFACE-- 11

INTRODUCTION--- 19

Chapter 1 RAISING YOUR VIBRATION ------------------------------------- 27

    Interview: Dr. George Pratt

Chapter 2 QUANTUM PHYSICS – OUR ENERGETIC WORLD -------- 55

    Interview: Charlie Rocket

Chapter 3 EMPOWERMENT THROUGH YOUR ENVIRONMENT --- 91

    Interview: Dr. Carolyn Daitch

Chapter 4 ORGANIZE AND ENHANCE YOUR SPACE ------------------ 133

    Excerpts: Marie Kondo team

Chapter 5 WHAT YOU CONSUME, CONSUMES YOU ------------------ 147

    Interview: MaryRuth Ghiyam

Chapter 6 MINDSET MATTERS--173

    Interview: David Meltzer

Chapter 7 COMMUNICATION TO CONNECTION -----------------------213

    Interview: Casey Adams

Chapter 8 ENHANCE YOUR BRAINWAVES--------------------------------241

    Interview: Dr. James Hardt

AFTERWORD --- 261

ACKNOWLEDGMENTS --- 265

REFERENCES --- 269

CONTRIBUTORS--- 271

FOREWORD

by

David Meltzer

David Meltzer is the co-founder of Sports 1 Marketing, and formerly served as CEO of the renowned Leigh Steinberg Sports & Entertainment agency, which was the inspiration for the movie *Jerry Maguire*.

He is a three-time international best-selling author, a Top 100 Business Coach, the executive producer of Entrepreneur's #1 digital business show, *The Two Minute Drill*, and host of the top entrepreneur podcast, *The Playbook*. David has been recognized by *Variety Magazine* as their Sports Humanitarian of the Year, and was awarded the Ellis Island Medal of Honor.

*

One of the greatest misconceptions people have is that we must constantly strive to "get happier". In reality, we all possess an innate capacity for happiness and joy. Instead of endlessly pursuing external sources of happiness, our focus should be on removing the barriers that hinder our connection to happiness, which also limits our true potential. In her book, *Happiness Habitat*, Jacqlyn Burnett shares valuable lessons that can help you eliminate these barriers, and experience a greater sense of happiness and fulfillment in all aspects of your personal and professional life. I can personally attest that Jacqlyn "walks the talk". She is one of the happiest people I know.

Being a part of this book is an honor for me because my life's mission is to empower over one billion people on Earth to find happiness. We have the ability to shape our own environment – a "happiness opportunity zone" – by surrounding ourselves with the right people, ideas, and activities. This requires regularly assessing our core values, and consistently making decisions that align with them. In this book, you will learn daily practices from top performers that can help you clarify your values, and make necessary changes to your routines and habits. By developing a system that empowers us to create new, positive habits, we can profoundly impact our connection to joy and happiness, because our habits shape our reality. This level of clarity also enables us to find balance in our lives; as knowing our values is key to finding our center, and swiftly returning to it. Even when challenging circumstances threaten to derail us.

Jacqlyn also highlights the importance of elevating our awareness to the people, ideas, and activities that bring us the most happiness. By paying attention to patterns that emerge over time, we can discern what truly works for us, and make any necessary adjustments. Once we understand the elements that bring us the most happiness, we are empowered to pursue them consistently, without giving up.

Regardless of where you are on your personal journey, there is always room for growth and improvement. *Happiness Habitat* equips you with the tools to elevate all

HAPPINESS HABITAT

aspects of your life, and harness your inner power to create extraordinary results. It also reminds you to celebrate your successes along the way, ensuring that you remain connected to your purpose, passion, and ultimately, your profitability.

Now, it is up to you to be kind to your future self, by performing acts of kindness, and clearing the interference between yourself and the happiness, that already resides within you.

PREFACE

Think about the happiest person you know; then ask yourself: "What makes this person so happy?" Now consider: "What are their characteristics?" Think about the environment they have created for themselves in their home life; their workspace; and their internal world, such as their mindset; and what they consume.

What makes *you* happiest? Think of a time when you experienced utter joy. Recall your environment; the people around you, the setting, and the action that brought you joy.

We all experience happiness in our own way, and that is the beauty of happiness; we create our own, what I call "Happiness Habitat". When we are happy, we are on center. And when we are on center all shortages, problems, and doubt become mere illusions. It's the understanding of how to bring yourself to operate and react from a center that's in equilibrium. This will unlock your true potential.

HAPPINESS HABITAT

Someone's Happiness Habitat can be viewed as everything that makes up that person's environment – from their mindset, health, communication, and everything in between. When you learn how to optimize your environment, you can then reach your true potential.

Happiness is a state of mind. Some people believe things that are *out there* will bring them happiness. But this is like a toddler with a new toy. It is fun for a while, then the happiness dissipates, and they need a new toy, then another, then another. This becomes a state of chasing happiness. True and ongoing happiness derives from when you feel great about yourself, whether or not you have a new toy. This is because true happiness starts from *within*. When you fully grasp this concept, your potential will be much more accessible, and soon you will be able to easily unlock your happiness and optimize your environment to reach it. And maintain it.

HAPPINESS HABITAT

Earlier I asked you to think about something that made you happy. Now think back to a time (or place) when you were on center, and happy. Reflect on what was happening and what was in your surroundings...

Now let's cross this bridge back to that feeling. Let's optimize your Happiness Habitat to help you better remain on center. Let's unlock and accelerate to accessing your full potential. Let's Optimize Your Opportunity Zone.

Before I go over how this book is going to expedite creating your own Happiness Habitat and truly Optimize Your Opportunity Zone, I'll first define "happiness" and "habitat":

hap·pi·ness

noun

—the state of being happy.

hab·i·tat

noun

—a person's usual or preferred surroundings.

HAPPINESS HABITAT

The state of being *happy* occurs when you realize how good things are. Your perspective creates this; it is the experience of when you are grateful for the present. The dictionary defines *habitat* as "a person's usual or *preferred* surroundings." Your surroundings contribute greatly to what defines you. Your habitat is within and without. Your Happiness Habitat is your zone to create whatever you desire, and to truly enjoy the journey.

My cousin and mentor, David Meltzer, defines happiness as "enjoying the pursuit of our potential." His journey through life has taught him many lessons about happiness... through both his struggles and his successes. He went from having $100 million in assets to losing everything. Then rebuilding it all over again, tenfold. The second time around, David was able to turn his failures into life lessons, then into fortunes through a process he calls, *Connected to Goodness* (the title of his first book). It was his ability to remove his ego-based emotions and build a foundation within that allowed him to create everything else around him. It was his understanding and awareness of the value he created within himself that allowed him to manifest and attract that same value everywhere else.

I've not only been able to learn through Dave from being family, but also through my career. I worked for Dave and his business partner, Hall of Fame quarterback, Warren Moon, at their company, Sports 1 Marketing, for a few years, starting in 2015, where I learned many invaluable lessons. One example is what Dave likes to call "the Dummy Tax": Learning through someone else's "struggle" rather than having to experience it on your own.

Perhaps the biggest lesson I've learned from Dave is to smile, not only through my triumphs, but also through my struggles, and failures. When we smile, and especially when we are grateful for what we have now, we are enhancing our alpha brainwaves. Dr. Jim Hardt, the pioneer in neurofeedback training, will explain the importance of these brainwaves later in this book.

HAPPINESS HABITAT

When we enhance our alpha, we enhance our creativity, problem solving ability, and we become solution oriented. And like a mirage, "struggle" just dissipates on the horizon of a new adventure for you.

No matter where you are on your journey, there will always be room for expansion. There will always be room to optimize. I'm going to show you how, and provide you with actionable methods to enhance your Happiness Habitat. Your habitat is your environment inside and out. Let's make our surroundings the best we possibly can in order to thoroughly enjoy our wonderful journey through life.

Through clarity we are able to see the beauty in this world. Whether you're just beginning your journey to a more enjoyable life, or you're already well on your way, this book is going to elevate your life in ways you couldn't even imagine. The terrific life you've always wanted is about to get a whole lot more beautiful. The space you've created for yourself is, in part, also going to be enhanced.

HAPPINESS HABITAT

Even if you're already reading this from your 30-acre estate on a cliff overlooking a twinkling ocean. This world has more than enough room for everyone to create the ideal life they desire. Life is all about finding the enjoyment of our present moment while embracing the pursuit of our potential. Let's do this. Let's create our Happiness Habitat. Starting now.

INTRODUCTION

The manifestation of my career, personal experiences and all that I've accomplished has been optimized through my Happiness Habitat. My journey has been a dynamic adventure. It hasn't always been a straight arrow, but I let my inner compass lead me in the direction of my passion.

In my earlier years at Michigan State University, I explored many aspects of my interests such as journalism, acting, and painting. After my "grooming" at Sports 1 Marketing, I worked for the youngest founder of a public traded company and self-made media mogul, Dan Fleyshman. There, I learned the mechanics of social media, viral campaigns, being an angel investor, then starting my own companies. I also learned to love the process in all efforts and give myself the opportunity to grow within my interests, all the while contributing to those around me, as well.

I became heavily invested in blockchain and cryptocurrency back in 2017, and built an IOS crypto emoji app (Crypto Emojis), mined bitcoin, and became Director of Operations for a blockchain company, Vezt. I was recognized as an expert in my field by Ryan Seacrest who interviewed me on KISS-FM, in order to help his listeners understand how blockchain works.

I've always had a passion for creating art. After I launched my digital agency, I connected with an art gallery owner, who saw my talents beyond my digital services. I created the opportunity to be showcased at his gallery, the W Hotel Hollywood Gallery, which lead to being shown in other galleries around the world.

Diving further into personal development, in 2019, I participated in the Deluxe Premium Double Alpha One Training at Biocybernaut, the pioneer of neurofeedback training. This groundbreaking practice promised and delivered Zen-like states in a matter of days, rather than the typical years.

My many years in the creator economy and business sector then best positioned me to serve as the Chief Operating Officer for what became the number one media kit tool, MediaKits. I was both the first employee and a founding member. After one year in business, in late 2022, we were acquired by Viral Nation, a powerhouse in the creator economy. It was an amazing thrill to build a company that caught the attention of so many people and organizations.

In 2023, I earned my certification as an Integrative Nutrition Health Coach. This multidimensional practice ties together elements of nutrition, mind, body, and spirit, furthering my dedication to comprehensive wellbeing.

Now, at the age of 29, my journey has led me to the most incredible places. I get to inspire and mentor others to step into their full potential. The underlying theme of my successes is an unwavering positive mindset, and a perpetual grateful perspective throughout my journey – in other words, my Happiness Habitat.

HAPPINESS HABITAT

I am absolutely in love with my environment that I've created for myself, and it has lead me to the here and now – sharing it with you. I am manifesting at a pace more rapid than ever before. And I have done so by shifting my mindset, environment, and everything in between. I am one of the happiest people I know, and I truly enjoy all that happens *through* me.

We get to experience the present once. It's a perfectly sent moment made up of our past actions, experiences, and emotions. Life is a gift; that's why we call our now the *present*. Here is the good news: We get to *create* our now. We get to experience life in the manner we aspire to, if we do it through intention and desire. I've done so through optimizing my Opportunity Zone, and I'm going to show you how to do the same.

My lens into this world comes from the feelings and emotions I have that allow me to enjoy this life to its fullest. I've been fortunate to have learned from some of today's great thinkers, who are going to share their lessons and techniques in this book, to Optimize Your Opportunity Zone. These experts, are not only pioneers in their respective fields, but are thought-leaders who have amounted their own success through creating *their* Happiness Habitat.

Happiness happens when we are inspired. When we are grateful for the present moment, we are happy. When we allow the interference of mostly ego-based emotions such as fear, doubt, anxiety, anger, being offended, or any of the negative feelings we have, we corrupt that connection. Your reactions when operating from this state of consciousness will cause your direction to deviate from what you want; which is happiness.

We all can become inspired; we all have the opportunity to operate at a higher vibration. This book will clear any interference to functioning at your true potential. David Meltzer has taught me this powerful lesson, which is the understanding for clearing any mental obstacles that stand in the way of experiencing joy. Optimizing your Opportunity Zone in all aspects of life will build the foundation for your Happiness Habitat.

Throughout this book you'll learn valuable lessons and exercises to expand your awareness from experts such as Dr. George Pratt. He is considered one of the leading clinical psychologists who focuses on high performance. MaryRuth, the creator of the best quality liquid vitamins on the market. Casey Adams, who has interviewed world-class individuals like Larry King, Robert Greene, Tyler Winklevoss, Rick Ross; and many more. My conversations with these experts detail their best practices for an enhanced life.

Life takes us through many experiences, or lessons. Everything that happens through us expands us. When we look for the light, love, and lessons in everything, we get to grow. Our lens defines how we experience this world, and what we have the power to create in it. Our universe has so much empty space. There's plenty of room for expansion.

When you operate from a place of happiness your lens is clear: To seeing opportunities, to the awareness of yourself, and those around you. And most importantly, how you experience the world. Your mindset dictates your perception, which dictates your reality. Its time to feed your consciousness with the right *nutrients* to maximize your opportunity. A simple way to expand your perspective to create a more abundant mindset is by simply changing your perspective. As the famous motivational speaker, Wayne Dyer, said: "Change the way you look at things, and the things you look at change." When you optimize your environment in your inner-world and your outer-world, you will be that much more inspired and effective.

The life I've created for myself is filled with joy, love, creativity, and pure harmony. I cannot remember the last time I wasn't able to get back to center in less than two minutes.

HAPPINESS HABITAT

This book is your blueprint to creating your dynamic zone for optimization and joy. You can only expand by having new data to operate with, and experiential knowledge to reflect on. I'm going to give you exactly this, what you need to live your most abundant life. Now, let's create your Happiness Habitat.

Chapter 1
RAISING YOUR VIBRATION

"Joy is what happens to us when we allow ourselves to recognize how good things really are."
—Marianne Williamson

Life is a beautiful thing. Your lens, or viewpoint, determines how you perceive this world. The higher frequency you operate on, the clearer your lens becomes. Raising your vibration literally means heightening your state of consciousness. Becoming more joyful. It's that feeling of lightness, gratitude, love, and empowerment.

Before we dive in, I'd like to check in with you: How are you feeling? Are you in a state of joy? Or could you raise your vibration? When you're on center and operating from your highest vibration you allow yourself to be in flow; aka in harmony. Take a moment to check in with yourself and notice how you're feeling. If you are not feeling completely on center, that's OK – I'm going to raise your vibration in the next few paragraphs.

When you are on center you have the opportunity to expand into the best possible version of yourself. When you operate from ego-based emotions such as fear, anger, or any type of stressful feeling, your body goes into survival mode. These types of emotions trigger your body's natural "fight or flight" response, which is driven from your sympathetic nervous system. All bodily systems are working to keep us alive in the perceived dangerous situation, rather than using the energy toward expansion.

During evolution, this type of response in the body was helpful when we felt threatened. When the threat went away, our body would return back it its natural, relaxed state.

However, in today's world, when there are ongoing negative emotions or stressors, your body is constantly in a heightened state. This type of feeling can be addictive as more adrenaline and cortisol is produced. But in reality your brain becomes narrower in its focus. In an actual threat, that needs your undivided attention, this would be helpful. But it is counterproductive when dealing with the everyday stressors of life.

You are in control of how you experience and react to every situation. Changing how you experience these situations will better keep you on center. Allow me to explain.

Your reality determines your perception of the world, or your lens. When you feel at your best, the situations that you experience become more positive than negative. Imagine going to dinner with your best friend at your favorite restaurant, right after you got a promotion in your workplace. That dinner is going to taste amazing, and the whole experience will likely be one of laughter and delight.

Now, imagine going to that same restaurant; but this time after a bad day at work, and with someone who really gets on your nerves. That dinner is going to taste a little duller.

Did you notice the nuance or meaning I attached to each experience? I framed your mindset in this first scenario as positive and rewarding. In the second scenario, I framed the situation as negative and perhaps even irritating. The meaning you attach to a situation will cause the experience you have to unfold in a likewise manner. In other words, changing how you perceive your "now" will change how you experience it.

In the "dull" dinner, let's take a moment and change the meaning and your perception to look for the light, love, and lesson in it. Notice how differently you might experience this dinner. Perhaps you even realize your day, and especially that person, were not all that bad. In fact, an opportunity for growth can come about from it because of your new perception. Why? Because you chose to look at the glass as half full, not half empty.

You can enhance and "clean" your lens by training yourself to adjust it to become clearer. Like a telescope, if the lens you are looking through has a little smudge, what you're looking at will be distorted. Your lens displays one moment at a time in a perfectly organized way. And the only time that exists is the here and now. Everything else is remembered or dreamed; your past or your future. Your now is made up of your past thoughts, emotions, and actions. You literally can only experience the present moment. Therefore, be grateful for the now, for you now know you can change it.

If you don't like your now, you can change your thoughts, change you attitude, change your behavior, and change how you react in situations – it's all a chain reaction. You have the power to change your now. The only person who can change your experience of how you experience the world is *you*. Be thankful for the present. It is a perfectly sent moment given to you to help you see the opportunities within and beyond.

I once went through a very traumatic experience and was having trouble shifting back to my center. I won't get too deep into this experience just yet (you will learn more in the coming chapters) but I'll share with you how it affected me for now. Not properly addressing traumas can shift your entire life experiences.

Back to this traumatic experience... I was allowing it to affect my focus in my career, and in my personal life as well. I was experiencing a feeling of lack. The usual extremely enjoyable experiences were shining a little less.

A mutual friend referred me to someone who could bring me back to center and even enhance my lens. This extraordinary human who helped me polish my lens was **Dr. George Pratt**. He taught me the techniques that would ultimately heal my trauma, and take me to a whole new state of supreme joy and high vibration.

Dr. Pratt is a licensed clinical and consulting psychologist with a private practice in La Jolla, CA. He specializes in psychotherapy, mind/body techniques, hypnotherapy, and performance enhancement. Dr. Pratt has a depth of training, and an abundance of experience, to help people relieve their perceived or actual difficulties, and work toward enhancement of their lives. He provides a wide range of treatment options for recovery from many forms of anxiety, depression, fear, and stress-related problems. Plus, tools and practices to enhance performance and effectiveness in business, athletics, academics, and other areas.

Dr. Pratt has worked with some of the best in their professions to enhance their lives, too. One such person is Rob Dyrdek. He is a TV personality, entrepreneur, producer, former professional skateboarder, and host of the show *Rob and Big*. Rob was feeling unfulfilled as a pro skateboarder. Rob worked with Dr. Pratt to literally get "hypnotized for success," as Rob has mentioned in some of his interviews. He went from being in a state of lack to being one of the best pro skateboarders in the industry, and gaining clarity and focus more than ever before. The results Rob has gained from working with Dr. Pratt have transformed his life, and the two of them have since built a long-standing relationship. I've also worked with Dr. Pratt many times, and he has enhanced my overall performance in life, and my enjoyment of it.

Dr. George Pratt is one of the greatest in his field. With over 30 years of experience, he works in a rapid and perceptive manner. Dr. Pratt has served as Chairman of Psychology, Scripps Memorial Hospital, La Jolla and has been on staff for over 25 years. He is a Fellow and Approved Consultant of the American Society of Clinical Hypnosis, and is Past-President of the San Diego Society of Clinical Hypnosis. He is a Diplomate of the Association for Comprehensive Energy Psychology, and the American Academy of Pain Management. He is also a member of several professional organizations including the American Psychological Association. Dr. Pratt served on the faculty of the University of Minnesota, and presently teaches at the University of California, San Diego Ext. He is co-author of three books: *CODE TO JOY: The Four-Step Solution to Unlocking Your Natural State of Happiness. INSTANT EMOTIONAL HEALING: Acupressure for the Emotions, A Clinical Hypnosis Primer.* And *HYPER-PERFORMANCE: Release Your Business Potential.*

The following is an interview I had with Dr. Pratt. In this conversation, he expands on his best practices for returning to your center, and how to enhance your life. I have adopted these exercises you're about to learn, and I invite you to try them as well.

> **Jacqlyn:** Dr. Pratt, I'm so grateful for how you've helped transform my life, and also for sharing your wisdom within Happiness Habitat. You are one of the most supreme psychologists and hypnotherapists, and I'm so grateful we've connected. Can you start by breaking down what you do?
>
> **Dr. Pratt:** I see a wide variety of clients. I've been doing it for quite a while, and I've used a variety of tools.

And yes, I'm a clinical psychologist and board-certified in hypnosis. I want to provide my clients with tools to help them accomplish their goals. So many psychologists just focus on problems. I am very good at helping fix problems. And then my goal was always to not just take somebody from a difficult position to neutral – but why stop there? We want to take them to enhancement and to success, and to accomplish their goals and objectives, and to have a wonderful time doing it.

Jacqlyn: Well, I can definitely agree with that! Can you walk me through the process of working together at a high level? I absolutely loved the process and it really helped me heal more than I could have imagined. It was literally transformational.

Dr. Pratt: What happens is I first take a history and we figure out what the true goals are. Now, for some people, let's say there was a terrible trauma they went through – and I've had kidnap cases and things like that. So many times people think, OK, I just want to get over this trauma. That's half of it, the person gets over the trauma. But then what do you want to do? Then you want to have a wonderful life. Whether it is in business, or accomplishing objectives, or sports, or doing fabulous work in any endeavor. We not only want to understand the problem, but what the goals are, and help them to clear any debris that's in the way, or associated with this.

Jacqlyn: You mentioned the importance of clearing traumas. Can you talk about this in terms of actually allowing a person to flow into their Optimization Zone?

Dr. Pratt: Yes, absolutely. When you came into the office, I showed you something that's called "energy psychology". Over the past few decades, it has been shown that it is possible to regain that childhood delight and live our lives to the fullest. As a result of this work, we have come to believe that we are here on this earth to be happy and healthy. And to experience joy, love, connection, and contribution. You can become a better, smarter, calmer, more focused, more powerful, and more deeply joyful you. For this to happen you need to clear this trauma and the fog of distress. We have spent the past several decades figuring out this puzzle using the tools of conventional psychology, along with new methods and insights from the latest findings at the cutting edge of a field of research and therapy, which is energy psychology. When you have those tools, it is very easy to unblock things, and achieve your goals.

We are all surrounded by a field of energy. And you want to use all those neurons. And we want you to use all of the body's energy system. And it is very, very powerful. I mean, we're talking about optimal performance in this situation. I have lots of professional athletes. I have a wide spectrum of folks. And I know that we can accomplish the objective for everybody that we see, if they do the process properly, even if it is long distance, or on their own.

Jacqlyn: I know the importance you've shared with me about having the right foundation, and the proper polarities to even begin to have the best optimization. And also implement your tools you talk about in your book that we've also worked on together. Can you expand on this?

Dr. Pratt: Many times, people will assume that with their self-reflection or their meditation, that they're going to be aligned. We are electrical beings. Therefore, we have polarity just like a copper-top battery. If that clarity is not right, even if you think it's right, it's not going to be, so people persuade themselves.

In my experience, many times they will say, "Oh, I already have that handled. I've already done some meditation on those things." Regardless of what you've done, the first step, if you don't have proper polarity, nothing is going to work. And that is shocking to them. "Well, I've been doing okay for the last five years." And we will do a little discussion, and they're kind of trying to persuade themselves that they're happy, when it's clear to me they are merely compensating.

As I said before, we're like copper-top batteries. The earth is negative, the bottoms of our feet should be positive and the top of our heads should be negative. And people are de-polarized frequently, particularly with stress, worry. I understand it, but they've artificially thought, "Well, I'm doing all these things, so I've got to be getting better." Then they come to me and they say, "Well, Rob Dyrdek, (or whoever referred them) said it helps, but I think I'm pretty fine." In reality, that person has only persuaded themselves that they are okay.

You are going to use much more of your capability when you're properly aligned, and with you using your subconscious mind as well. The conscious mind is 20 to 40 neurons firing per second at the subconscious. Also called the unconscious level, it's 20 to 40 million neurons firing per second. If you are just doing this consciously, you're getting a tiny bit of benefit. But it is much more powerful when you include the unconscious, and that's why hypnosis can be very helpful. And that's why other tools that use the body's energy system can be very useful. Then once they experience that, it's like opening a floodgate of new positive energy.

Jacqlyn: How can you be thrown off polarity?

Dr. Pratt: If you're dealing with a frustration, or a trauma, or a block about success or achieving your goals, you're probably going to have that inverse polarity.

Jacqlyn: What are some of the tools that use the body's energy system that can properly set the foundation, and realign the body's energy system?

Dr. Pratt: Number one, we are going to do something called "balanced breathing". That's a two-minute technique. The second technique is called "grounding". It will help you to feel more present and in your body. Sometimes we can become so stressed that we almost feel like we're not in our bodies. This technique will help you get grounded. The third technique is we are going to stimulate an energy center on your body that will help with polarity. And it will help calm you as well.

The first technique is balanced breathing. Now, this is a technique that will help calm you. It will help calm your central nervous system. We know that we have a parasympathetic nervous system and a sympathetic nervous system. The parasympathetic calms us down. It is the state that all healing exists in. The sympathetic gears us for taking action, or for fight-flight or freezing. We want to activate the parasympathetic and calm us down.

Put your left ankle over your right, and right hand out over your left, then interlock your fingers. And you can either rotate your hands to your chest or you can leave them in your lap. This is also a two-thousand-year-old meditation.

For about two minutes, tongue to the roof of your mouth as you breathe, then relax the tongue as you exhale. Tongue up, breathe in. Relax the tongue, breathe out.

Now, we are electrical. Again, we are like a copper-top battery. We have a positive, and we have a negative. When you pass electrical current, you create polarity. These three techniques depend on that.

The second thing that we're going to do is grounding. This is going to help you to feel present, to feel your feelings a little more clearly, and help prevent something like orbiting your body. Just sit back and put your feet on the floor, put your hands on the abdomen, and then close your eyes. Now, I want you to imagine feeling connected to the center of the Earth. You're feeling a connective cord between your abdomen and the center of the Earth that is going to help you to feel more clearly. Just breathe in, and you don't have to do anything special with your tongue. But always breathe deep, that always helps, too. Just *feel* you are connected to the center of the Earth.

The third tool involves stimulating an energy center on the body. It's about halfway between your left collarbone and left nipple. It's about right in the middle of the Pledge of Allegiance position. First, flatten your hand. Then rub the spot clockwise as though a clock is sitting on your chest. And as you do so, think or say out loud, and repeat, a statement such as, "I deeply love and accept myself. I deeply love and accept myself. I deeply love and accept myself. I deeply love and accept myself. I deeply love and accept myself. I deeply love and accept myself. I deeply love and accept myself. I deeply love and accept myself. And I deeply love and accept myself."

Again, whether you say this out loud, or just think it, the process will help correct polarity imbalance. You'll feel calmer after you do that.

Jacqlyn: Wonderful, Dr. Pratt. I absolutely enjoy these practices, and really feel the difference in my whole being when I'm doing them.

Dr. Pratt: Sure, that's some of the concepts, particularly from my most recent book called *Code to Joy*. Many of our challenges have blocks from the subconscious that are the result of growing up in families that might have dismissed you, or you didn't feel loved. You have to clear those issues too, so that you don't feel blocked for success. If you and your inner state feel that you love yourself, that's a big step. If you feel like you are kind of trying to force yourself to do it – let's say you've had an upbringing or family that's been dysfunctional in some way – you have to clear those patterns.

Otherwise, it's a bit like spray-painting on rust. That's so you'd just look good. You want to feel good.

Jacqlyn: If you're unsure about blockages or traumas, what is a good way to identify this?

Dr. Pratt: Identify what your goals are, then write a note to yourself: "Why haven't I gone through these issues?" You do a little personal inventory to direct you to what the problems are.

I've worked with plane crash survivors, and all sorts of difficult situations, so the process and methods I listed earlier works at the therapeutic level. But it's also for everyday sorts of things, to help you achieve your goals, be happier at home, or at work. They are wonderful, all-purpose tools.

We are using the unconscious mind in a different way. We want to have the foundation so you are seeing clearly. You don't want to be driving down the

> Autobahn at 160 miles an hour and your windshield is all messy. You want to turn on your windshield wipers so you can see clearly.
>
> **Jacqlyn:** Thank you so much Dr. Pratt. I appreciate you sharing your expertise and counsel for living a more enhanced life.

As you now know, it is very important to set the proper foundation prior to adjusting any other practices. To get the full benefit of them moving forward, your polarity must be aligned. Now that we have set your foundation and enhanced your current state of being, next we are going to focus on the continuation of raising your vibration.

As you move throughout this journey, you need not be certain of your future, as you literally cannot see beyond the now. Instead, focus on the mission, your beliefs and your goals, and the road will create itself. You can be certain of the present as that is the only moment that exists. That's not to say you do not have a plan. A plan is merely the alignment of the pursuit to your mission. There's no need to fear the uncertain; for uncertainty is where the new and creative are born. Be grateful for the unknown as you get to grow within it.

Imagine driving at dusk with your headlights off. You know your destination, but you can only see a few yards in front of you. This is how life works. You know your mission, beliefs, and goals, but the journey of a concrete path to what you desire might be unknown. Perhaps there are some speed bumps and even a flat tire along the way. By operating on a premium tank of gas rather than diesel, this will help you get to your destination that much more quickly, and make it more enjoyable.

I'm here to help you raise your vibration and be your guide to performing on that premium fuel. Raising your vibration, being in joy, and operating from a place of happiness adds to your flow, and creates a larger opportunity to operate at your full potential.

HAPPINESS HABITAT

Happiness for me is defined as being grateful for the present moment. When you're grateful for the present your lens is that much clearer, no smudge to be found. I wake up every morning and take an action where my lens is clear; an action where I am vibrating at my highest frequency. This might be a gratitude exercise, a warm blissful shower, or even calling my mom (she's a true beaming light of joy). Once I start my day with a high-frequency action, everything from there is a reaction. When I get off center, I remind myself of the feeling I had when I was on center, and I return to a state of flow.

Let's do a couple exercises now.

EXERCISE 1

It doesn't matter what time of day it is. Recall a memory, moment, or activity that truly brings you utter joy. Think of what you felt like when you experienced this.

Just by sheer remembering, you put your mind back in that state, a higher vibration. It's just like smiling. Even if you are going through a struggle, through smiling you will release more serotonin. This is a natural chemical that is produced in our body. It transmits messages between nerve cells, and contributes to wellbeing and happiness, among other things. You can create the feeling of increased joy just by thinking about how it feels.

Take time here, now, to close your eyes and practice this exercise – recall a situation, event, or moment that has brought you happiness – and if you'd like, smile while doing so.

EXERCISE 2

Another way to increase joy and raise your vibration is through practicing gratitude. What is gratitude? The affirmation of goodness. Happiness also happens when you realize how good things really are. It is seeing the potentiality within. By truly appreciating what you have, and giving or receiving gratitude, you can raise your frequency.

HAPPINESS HABITAT

One other aspect to gratitude is that just by simply observing gratitude you can gain benefits, too. Acknowledging what you are grateful for, giving or receiving gratitude, and also witnessing gratitude (i.e., seeing someone receive or give another a compliment) is another way to release serotonin.

Serotonin raises your vibration and is a counterpart to remaining in flow. Imagine your whole body as a river flowing freely. That's when your body is operating at its highest frequency.

Now imagine in that river there are a few thick tree branches and boulders. As a result, the river isn't running so freely; some of the water is even getting trapped in a few areas. This in turn slows the rest of the river down. In real life, this is a blockage of your energy and your own flow. When you set the foundation, practice gratitude, and truly raise your vibration, you allow flow and optimization for the rest of your being.

HAPPINESS HABITAT

Every single moment of the day we get to make a decision of how we react and behave. It is your duty to be the best version of yourself. Operating from a place of love, gratitude, and light will have you performing as your finer self. Life can either happen to you, or through you. When you see life as happening *to* you, you are not being accountable; and you trap those negative emotions that feed the blockages and shortages; thus, you block the connection to that which inspires you.

When you understand that life happens *through* you, you allow yourself to grow in multiples. If you look for the light, love, and lessons in all you encompass, you will continue expanding.

For the next week, begin your day with an activity or action that brings you joy. If you need to, write it down, take a picture, or capture this moment however you'd like, to record your findings. Go on with your day observing yourself and your emotions. Whenever you feel like you are starting to go

HAPPINESS HABITAT

off-center, pause and recall the moment
when you started your day with the activity
that brought you to center, and to joy.

Chapter 2
QUANTUM PHYSICS – OUR ENERGETIC WORLD

"The physical world is literally made up of ideas and energy."
—*David Cameron Gikandi*

Your entire being and experience of a flow state are constantly in symbiosis with the rest of the world. So, what does this have to do with quantum physics?

Quantum physics is the study of how energy behaves at the subatomic level. All matter is made up of subatomic particles, which are constantly interacting with each other in a wave-like manner. This means that everything in the universe is interconnected and indivisible. Your thoughts, ideas, and emotions also create invisible waves that interact with one another; similar to how radio waves transmit information. Just as sound has a vibration, your thoughts and emotions also have a vibrational frequency.

HAPPINESS HABITAT

By examining the principles of quantum physics, you can gain a deeper understanding of the interconnected nature of reality, and how it relates to flow. Quantum physics helps us understand how the matter of all things is created, and functions in relation to the rest of the universe. Understanding how the fundamental building blocks of the universe operate can provide insights into how to cultivate and enhance the state of flow in your own life. By harnessing the power of quantum physics to optimize flow, you can significantly enhance your well-being, and achieve unparalleled levels of productivity and satisfaction.

Understanding how something functions, and what it is composed of, can provide insight into its purpose, and how to use it effectively. When you have a clear understanding of your actions, thoughts, and ideas, you can more confidently and effectively materialize them. For example, having a solid execution plan is essential for the success of launching a new business. Without a well-defined strategy and plan, your confidence and ability to launch this business may be diminished.

I mentioned that quantum physics is the study of how energy behaves at the subatomic level. From humans to plants, rocks, plastic, and everything in between, we all are at the foundation made up of tiny little particles. A body is made up of cells, which are made up of molecules, which are composed of atoms, which are made up of subatomic particles. The thing that makes you different from anything else is how these particles are put together. That's right, you live in a quantum world. Learning how to optimize in this world can aid in your own materialization for anything you desire.

If every thought and emotion carries a quantum particle, or functions as a wave, it's possible to envision how these waves interact with each other in the universe. Imagine a pond where you throw a pebble, creating a ripple effect. If another pebble is thrown into the pond, the ripples will combine to create a larger wave. This is where the concept of

HAPPINESS HABITAT

"manifesting" comes into play. Manifesting is the generation of intention and desire. It's not about magically conjuring up a red Porsche on your driveway just by wishing for it. Rather, it's about being intentional with your actions, and genuinely desiring something, then aligning your manifestation with similar quantum waves in order to bring it closer to reality.

How can you attract more of what you want in your life? It's by harnessing your thoughts, productively communicating, and getting to know your energetic self.

Thoughts

Did you know that the average person has over 40,000 thoughts per day? That's a lot of opportunities to shift your perspective and choose positivity. Even the most confident individuals can fall victim to negative or fear-based thinking. But don't let that stop you. You have the power to change your thoughts and take your power back. By observing yourself in the third person, you can train your subconscious to dictate your conscious thoughts. Imagine watching yourself from the corner of the room. This detachment allows you to look at your thoughts objectively, and let negative ones pass by. Remember, "what you resist persists", so embrace the power of positivity and watch your life transform.

The more positive thoughts you focus on, the more you'll attract those kinds of thoughts into your life. It's all about vibrational frequency – like attracts like. The first step to changing those repetitive or negative thoughts is to become aware of them. Take note of what kinds of thoughts dominate your consciousness. If you notice a thought that does not serve you, simply observe it, allow it to pass, and then release it. Or, you can reflect on why it is there, then move on. Either way, the key is to become aware of your thoughts, and choose to focus on the ones that will bring positivity and success into your life.

If you look at yourself from a bird's-eye view, or third-person perspective, you can gain a new level of awareness and control over your thoughts. This detachment allows you to observe your thoughts objectively, and choose which ones to focus on. By practicing this skill, you can break free from repetitive or negative thought patterns, and open yourself up to new positive possibilities. Try using the exercise at the end of this chapter to make thought observation a part of your daily routine.

My oldest and dearest friend, Lisa Kent, is an outstanding Holistic Practicing Psychotherapist. I'm lucky that she's frequently enlightening me with her experiential knowledge. One of these focuses are on the relationship between manifestation and thoughts. As Lisa has taught me, your thoughts are closely connected to your emotions, and play a crucial role in determining your ability to manifest.

For instance, when you hold limiting beliefs, such as feeling unworthy of abundance, this negativity seeps into your thoughts and emotions. This negativity not only affects your emotions, but also your energy and vibration, making it difficult to manifest your desires. Conversely, when you adopt positive thoughts and emotions of abundance, and belief in your own worthiness, your energy and vibration are positively impacted, thus making it easier to manifest your desires.

Manifestation is not just about what you want, but also what you believe. Your thoughts have a profound impact on your emotions and your ability to manifest. It is important to be mindful of the thoughts you are allowing to take root in your mind. By shifting your thoughts toward positivity, and belief in your own worthiness, you can harness the power of manifestation to bring your desires to fruition.

Communication

When you start believing in yourself and your abilities, you'll find that things start to "manifest" or align in your favor much easier. This is because manifestation involves not only your thoughts and beliefs, but also the communication you have with yourself. By changing the way you talk to yourself, and the thoughts you focus on, you can set the stage for positive change.

Charlie Jabaley, also known as **Charlie Rocket**, is an excellent example of the power of belief and manifestation. He is one of my dear friends and a true inspiration to me. Charlie is an absolute all-star, having managed Grammy-nominated and winning artist 2 Chainz. Within just two years, he lost 135 lbs., ran 3 marathons, reversed the growth of a brain tumor, and became an Ironman. Shortly after, he embarked on a Dream Machine bike tour across America. He was featured in *Runner's World* magazine, and secured a partnership with Nike. Charlie's story has inspired countless people. He now spends most of his time on his mission: To transform millions of people worldwide.

HAPPINESS HABITAT

I sat down with Charlie to dive more into what it means to manifest, and the understanding of quantum physics.

Jacqlyn: Charlie, you're a true master of the quantum world. You literally manifested where you are today! Can you please help me understand quantum?

Charlie: Have you heard the saying, "When the student is ready, the teacher appears?" My whole life I was in the music game. I never knew anything else. I got in as a teenager, and then I got sick. But when I left music and began losing weight, all this crazy stuff started happening so frequently that I was scared to tell people. I didn't want them to think I was weird. But it would be literally not just one time a day, not just two times a day, but like five, six times a day. And it was so much I started making a list on my phone about, "What do I mean by 'crazy stuff'?"

HAPPINESS HABITAT

I'm from Atlanta. I remember there was this time I was running down the Strand, and I thought of somebody I hadn't thought of in ten years. Her name was Sansore. It just hit me out of nowhere. So, I went on Instagram. And when I knew her, there wasn't even an Instagram. I tried to find her. But I didn't remember exactly how to spell Sansore. I tried six, seven different accounts. It wasn't her, so I gave up. And then, the next day, *she* DMd me. I got the DM on my phone.

I literally could pull it up. I'm like, "Look, I was searching for you yesterday." It was just super crazy.

Certain things like I was working on this deal... And when you're doing a deal with somebody, you know, you'll negotiate the number. Let's say the number was one hundred and thirty thousand. Once you negotiate the number, your attorneys are going back and forth, locking it in. One morning I was in the shower. I remember, it was Thanksgiving morning, and I had a feeling... *They're going to give me more money.* I literally felt it. A couple hours later, I get a phone call from their attorney who said, "We want to add thirty thousand dollars to it." I'm thinking, *That just doesn't happen!* But at the same time, "I knew..." It sounded crazy, but, "I was in my shower, and I just had a feeling!"

Then there's things around the same time where I would write down in my notebook, – I journal – that I'm going to be in a commercial with LeBron James or Serena Williams. And I want to be a Nike athlete. I just had the vision, and I believed, and I'm very delusion-ally optimistic about my dreams. And, as you know, a few months later, I was in one of the biggest commercials that ever existed. You know, Nike commercials. The Colin Kaepernick commercial created billions of dollars in revenue for Nike's culturally pivoting... It's just crazy.

With quantum physics, when all these crazy things started happening in my life – like constantly – this guy came into my life. He overheard me speaking, and he said, "You're very quantum." I'm like, "What does that mean?" Because I had never heard of quantum physics. And Mr. Collier said, "I could tell by the way you talk, the confidence, and how you speak, and how you say things about the future is as if they're already done."

Mr. Collier went on to say, "My guess is you're experiencing a lot of magic right now in your life." I said, "Man, you have no idea." I pulled out my phone, showed him the list. Mr. Collier said, "Let me teach you about this." And I was able to piece it all together from the knowledge. It was because I cleaned up, and I got to a place where I was vibrating in a way that I felt like I was connected to this universe. To where I could say something, and Boom! Or I could just know something.

So, part of it is knowing the future, because I'm connected to the knowledge, because in the quantum field, there's no space or time. Here in this just 3D world we're living in, time is one, two, three... day... day... hour... hour... minute. But I would know what's next. And I would also be able to connect to what I wanted to create what was next; and it's the most powerful I've ever felt in my life.

I was eating high frequency food. Food that is alive. High vibrational food. I'm now kind of known to my friends and following as a dreamer, almost like a magician or a wizard. And my secret is, I believe in the dream so much that I'll close my eyes, and I'll play it out in a million different ways to where I feel it so much... I'll give you the example: I wanted to be the Nike athlete, right?

I wanted to make a fan-made Nike commercial. But what I wanted to make was the actual real Nike commercial, not like some little Instagram clip. So, I started calling my Hollywood television producer friends. I'd say, "Okay, this is what I'm looking for. I'm looking for somebody who can film, owns really good equipment, anamorphic lenses. And I need them to be able to make music, because I want to do this Hans Zimmer style music. And I need them to be good at DaVinci and color grading. And I need them to be able to mix and master the audio for the voiceover." The television producer friends all said variations of, "Charlie, that's like seven different people." They'd ask, "What's your budget for this?" I'd say, "I don't really have much of a budget for this. I just have to find this person who could do all of it." They'd say, "Charlie, you can't find that person. That person doesn't exist." I'm like, "Nah, there's somebody who could do all of that." They'd say, "Charlie, be realistic! What you want to make is going to cost over $60,000."

It needed to be Nike level, and I knew Nike films are usually a $200,000 or $300,000 budget, upwards to millions. I don't like it when people tell me to be realistic. I actually got mad. I got frustrated. I started speaking extremely confidently to anyone who told me to be realistic. I'd say, "Watch what I'm about to do!" I'm telling them the future. "I'm about to find this. Don't tell me I can't do it." I have a fire inside me. I just don't like being told I can't do something.

That's when I learned about the power of a word. I said, "I'm going to find him tomorrow. Watch!" Our word is our wand. Abracadabra means "As I speak, I create." That's the meaning of the word. As I speak, I create. We're the only mammal that can speak, and that's why we are creators. We create because we have the word. I was living in Santa Monica at the time. I pulled out my notebook. And I'm writing in my notebook, like delusionally writing, "I expect magic. I expect a miracle to happen."

In life, you receive what you're prepared for. If you're prepared for something bad to happen, or if you're prepared for a miracle to happen, either way you're right. And that's what you're going to receive. So, I wrote down, "Today is the day I searched and found my videographer/editor. It's done. Exclamation mark! It's easy. Exclamation mark!" That's what I wrote. And two hours later, my roommate walks in the front door. My roommate, Morgan, not a very exciting guy, just an accountant, works at

Whole Foods. But behind him is a guy holding this massive camera rig. I asked, "Morgan, why is there a camera guy following you?" He said, "Well, I just got a phone call from my friend, Manny. He's got this Airbnb business, and he wanted to film something at the house. So, he sent over the camera guy." I'm sitting there on the couch. And this camera guy walks in the front door, and I'm thinking, *Maybe, this is my guy? Maybe, this is the miracle?*

But when I looked closely at this camera guy, I lost a little bit of hope. He's very gothic, and I'm very inspirational and colorful. He's wearing all black, just hair all over his face. And I'm thinking, *I don't know about this guy, but let me talk to him.* So, I said, "Hey, man! What's your name?" He says, "My name is Adrian." And he just sounded sad. But I said, "All right! Do you do video work?" He said, "Yeah, I do video work, but nobody ever pays me." Then he went on a rant: "The only reason why I'm doing this video is because there was a Lamborghini, and I just wanted to look at the cool car." I said, "Whoa, whoa, whoa! Let me see some of your work." But he sounded just so negative, like a very depressed human being. So now I'm thinking, *This can't be my guy. He walked in my front door, but he can't be my guy.*

But what the heck. I pulled up his website he told me about. And it all went Boom! I click on this short film, and I'm astounded. "Man, did you shoot this?" He said, "Yeah, I shot it." I said, "This is amazing! Whose equipment did you use, because this is some of the most cinematic footage I've ever seen!" He said, "Well, I'm kind of like a hoarder. Anytime I make money, I buy camera equipment. And I just keep buying camera equipment." I asked, "Who edited this?" He said, "Well, I edited it too." I said, "All right." Then I said, "Man, this music!

This music is unbelievable." Filmmakers usually aren't good at making music. They either go on a royalty-free website, or if you're in the film industry, you pay hundreds of thousands of dollars for Hans Zimmer to make an original score. And the score is what makes the film. That's what makes being a great filmmaker difficult.

I asked, "Who did this music, because this isn't like royalty-free stuff?" He said, "Well, I used to be in a rock band. We were on the Warped Tour, had a record deal. I'm a musician, but the record label dropped us, and we're not famous anymore." I said, "Oh, man, like this is absolutely amazing. Who did the mixing and mastering of this voiceover?" He said, "Well, I have a recording studio in my bedroom. So, I'm kind of like a geek. I just like making everything sound good." I asked, "Who did the color grading on this? This is the richest footage." He said, "Well, I taught myself DaVinci." I mean, my mind was blown. He just walked in my front door. So, I said, "Adrian, do you need a job?" He said, "I applied to Hulu a couple of weeks ago, and they wouldn't even hire me." Nobody would hire him.

I said, "Adrian, I'll hire you right now. Look, this is what we're gonna do. We're going to make a fan-made Nike commercial. And Nike's going to see it, and Nike's gonna want to sign me as their athlete." He laughed. "Man, you're crazy." I shook my head. "No, no, no! I know this is gonna happen. I know this is gonna happen." I showed him my notebook. I said, "Look, I just wrote about you. And you walked in my front door. This is divine. When we make this Nike commercial, they're gonna want to sign me."

And so we sat down at a restaurant. We kind of made a vision board, and we put it out. And thanks to Casey

Adams, it went viral. Nike called me three days later. And I became a Nike athlete, and then the biggest Nike commercial of all time.

It really came down to belief. Knowing it was already done. Knowing that time just hadn't kind of caught up yet. And when there's disbelief, I always say, "Dream crazy and believe bigger." The reason why I say "dream crazy" is because the crazy dreams are easier than the realistic ones. Think about it. At times in my life when I've tried to do realistic things, I've experienced so much more friction. But when I've dreamed so big, there's seemed to be some force outside of me that helps me. And I look at it as a ripple back from the quantum field.

Let's think about a pool, for example. If I were to put my pinky toe in a pool, that'd create the smallest little wave, and that wave would just disappear before it even got to the side of the pool. But if I cannonball into the pool, a massive wave ripples throughout the entire pool, but then it bounces back to me. And that's me receiving the wave. I created a wave, but that wave comes back. And being bold is easier than being busy. I've done both. Both work. Don't get me wrong. There are miracles, and the miracles are from something very intelligent. And I believe that there's a force. It's almost like a video game. And we can play it. And there are cheat codes that we can play. If we're going through this life and we unlock our cheat codes, then I believe like when I started learning about quantum physics. That explains what the religions and the yogis and the mystics have been saying for thousands of years.

In the past, science was always separate from religion or mystics. But now, science says, "Okay, yeah, there is something else that's not exactly explainable, up until recent modern science since the mid-1900s." It is now explaining that there's magic and that information can travel faster than the speed of light. That atomic particles are connected, even at an unlimited distance. And there is a lot going on in between the space of me and you. They just haven't created the camera yet. Soon, they'll create the camera, just like they created an X-ray where they could see inside of our body. One day, they're going to create a camera and it will show us what's going on in between us because we're not separate. We're all connected. And all the experiments that have been conducted come back to saying, "Our heart is what unlocks the magic and our belief, when we get our mind to connect with our heart." Because usually, they are at war with each other. Usually, my heart says, "I wanna be a Nike athlete." And then, my head says, "Try to be realistic." But our head is so powerful. Our head is the only thing that can play tricks on us. So we've got to tame it and get it in alignment.

There's a lot of things that try to pull us out of that magical frequency. It might be a toxic person in our life, such as somebody you work for, a co-worker, or a family member. And it takes us out of the magic. But if we can tune our frequency, a lot like you tune a radio station, for example... In quantum physics, everything is a wave. That's one of the biggest discoveries in modern science: That everything is vibrating, that a very little percentage of the atomic particle is matter, 99.99 percent is energy. But if it has some energy, that means it's a wave. If it's a wave, that means it's not right here. It's spreading out throughout the entire pool. So, think about a rock dropping into a pool. The rock is so small in comparison to the reach that the waves have. So, if I'm a wave and you're a wave, that means we're able to connect somewhere out there. But we've got to realize that is very similar to the radio. You can't receive unless you tune.

Let's take a radio, for example. A radio in the old-school form is called a receiver, just like your phone is a receiver. And this receiver has a knob on it. And if I'm tuned to 99.3, but there's no radio station at 99.3, all I hear is static. There's nothing there. But if I just tune to a certain frequency, all of a sudden it pulls a perfectly clear, crisp sounding, orchestrated song out of the air. The song was always in the air. How many songs are flying past your face right now that you don't know? They're in the waveform. Not until you tune to it. And it doesn't even miss a note. How does a song fly through the air? I mean, if we were to go back hundreds of years ago, they would say this is witchcraft. This is not real. There's got to be little people inside the radio playing it. But how many phone conversations are flying past our faces right now? But the phone automatically tunes to receive.

For us and our dreams, all we have to do is, through meditation, through belief, through connecting our heart with our mind, believe that is what's meant for us, and to speak it and to feel it. And through that process, you start aligning with your dreams, or aligning with something you need, or aligning with a miracle. And you receive just like the radio.

Jacqlyn: Thank you for enlightening me, Charlie. That was beautiful.

Energetic Self

Subatomic particles, as you've learned, are the building blocks of our entire makeup. Although, you don't end at your physical body, you exist way beyond it. Imagine the steam coming off of a shirt after a steam press; the wrinkles dissipating are like energy rising. You know when you are in that flow state. There's absolutely no price tag you can put on the feeling of being in flow, because of the impact of change it has: How you produce results, intimacy, love, contribution, etc. It is the state of superfluidity. There's no viscosity. It's when the friction is gone. Athletes know this feeling quite well. It is the state that got them to that hole-in-one, a game-winning touchdown, or those timeless moments as they performed at their peak potential. When you are in this effortless state, you are the most receptive to being able to receive and download everything around you. If you want to spend more time in this space, you need to optimize your body to be open to it.

Dr. John Amaral (somatic energy practitioner) is the leader in this space. Dr. Amaral helps optimize the body to be in this energetic state. I've worked with Dr. Amaral many times to release any of the "wrinkles" aka bound-up energy and blockages in my body, to optimize my flow. Dr. Amaral is a pioneer in his field and has worked with some of the most influential entertainers and entrepreneurs to align and clear their energy. His clients include Gwyneth Paltrow, Tony Robbins, and Julianne Hough, to name a few. Optimizing your energetic self can catapult you into having more energy, enhance your confidence, and help clear traumas to allow your body to flow more freely.

Dr. Amaral works with the energetic body to introduce new possibilities for how the brain and body pay attention. "Energy is real, and it makes up everything – from our bodies to the universe as a whole. In fact, the universe is made up of more than 96% energy, and only about 4% physical matter. The Energy Flow Formula is about cultivating your awareness of the energy within and around you and learning how to use it." (johnamaral.com/faq). When you increase energy and awareness, the whole body can transform.

According to Dr. Amaral, when you have tension, aches, or scars, it's there as a result of trapped energy in the body. When there is trauma in the body, you can think of this as a large boulder in a river, preventing the water from flowing freely. Likewise, preventing you from reaching your true potential.

I'll share with you an example of the power of energy and transformation, although it's not a particularly pleasant one. In 2017, I was on set filming a campaign for a brand. One scene involved using a large pitcher of hot water. As I went to fill the pitcher, the hot water suddenly exploded, shattering the glass. The shards of glass fell mostly around me, but one piece landed on my big toe, causing it to go numb. A week later, my toe was still numb, a scar was forming, and I was still barely able to walk with my left foot. I decided to visit the doctor again. He told me there was a possibility the feeling in my toe would never come back because the nerves were so damaged.

It wasn't until I started working with Dr. Amaral in 2019 that I learned it didn't have to be this way. There was built-up tension locked in the scar tissue of my toe, and Dr. Amaral helped me release it. At first, I was skeptical, as I had never experienced an energetic phenomenon before. Although the doctor had told me the feeling in my toe might never come back, I remembered what my good friend, Garrain Jones, once told me: "You can't receive with your hands closed." So, I remained open to the possibility that the feeling could return.

This is how I successfully used the power of energy and transformation: Dr. Amaral had me close my eyes and put my hands over my numb toe. Then he told me to release a loud sound that I felt resonated with the scar tissue in my numb toe.

You might be wondering, *What kind of noises are you talking about?* That is exactly what I thought when Dr. Amaral instructed me to take this action. At first, I felt awkward yelling at a body part of mine. But Dr. Amaral made me feel comfortable by joining in and leading the way. I allowed myself to fully express the noise of the trauma trapped in my affected area. It didn't matter if I thought the noise was right or wrong. On key or off key. The goal was to just imagine what it would sound like if the trauma could make noise, and then make it.

It wasn't until that moment that I had ever felt a sensation in my toe. I realized then just how powerful the mind and body can be when you believe in your own strength – as Charlie had mentioned earlier. As the numbness left my toe and a sense of "home" returned, I was able to experience an energetic phenomenon for the first time in my life.

So, why did Dr. Amaral ask me to make that noise? And how could it possibly help me regain feeling in my toe? As he explained, our bodies are made up of subatomic particles, and the sounds we make carry vibrations. These vibrations can alter the patterns of our cells, and promote healing. Have you ever heard a sound that was extremely unpleasant – like someone screaming at the top of their lungs – that made you feel uneasy? Or have you ever listened to music that brought a sense of peace throughout your body? For me, one of those songs is *Clair de Lune,* or anything by Michael Bublé. By mimicking the noise of the affected, traumatized area, I was able to release the trapped cell pattern.

This was the first time I personally experienced the energetic world in a whole different way. In 1985, neuroscientist Dr. Candace Pert published groundbreaking research showing that emotions can trigger peptides to carry chemical messages throughout the body, and chemically change the cells. The emotions that I released in that instance allowed me to physically alter my cells. The same way my emotions and the cut triggered the numbness in my toe, I was able to use my emotions and energy to influence my cells to realign.

I was able to experience this phenomenon because I was open to the possibility. Prolonged negative emotions can create physical traumas in the body and vice versa. For example, the constant stressors in life can take a toll on physical health. We've all heard the expression "You're going to give me a heart attack!" Emotions and physical health are interconnected. That's why doctors often ask about recent emotional or traumatic events. Many physicians now recognize trauma as a factor in overall well-being. Chronic physical discomfort often stems from emotional trauma that has not been properly healed. By being aware of this, you can use your emotions as tools to influence your cells.

Understanding the connection between flow, quantum physics, and manifesting is crucial for achieving optimal well-being, and productivity. By embracing the principles of quantum physics, you can gain insight into how to cultivate and enhance the flow state in your life. Aligning your thoughts, emotions, and ideas with similar quantum waves through the practice of manifesting, and adopting a positive mindset, can attract more of what you want in your life. Focus on the good, and that will continue to be actualized. The power of your thoughts, emotions, and ideas is boundless.

By being *intentional* in your actions, genuinely desiring something, and aligning your manifestation with similar quantum waves, you can bring your desires into your reality. It's time to take control of your thoughts, optimize your flow state, and manifest your dreams to become reality.

EXERCISE 3

Let's revisit the section about thoughts. Your thoughts are extremely powerful. They fuel your actions, ideas, and they are the means to how you remember life. You have over 40,000 thoughts a day. Many of those thoughts are repetitive, and in many cases negative. You might not even realize it! This exercise will help you improve on experiencing the good life by auditing your thoughts.

First, know that your thoughts have a vibration, and the frequency you operate on attracts like vibration. Therefore, it's a good idea to become aware of these thoughts, so you can influence the good, and can keep attracting the great.

HAPPINESS HABITAT

An effective way to do this is by observing and auditing your thoughts. To do this, imagine yourself from the third person. It's like watching yourself from a bird's-eye view. Imagine looking at yourself from another point of the room, or another perspective. You will find it will be easier to detach from your thoughts by observing yourself this way. Once you get really good at this, you'll subconsciously observe your thoughts automatically.

Step 1: This is a five-minute exercise. You are going to take these next few minutes to observe yourself in the third person, or bird's-eye view. Get yourself situated wherever you are comfortable, and have a timer ready.

Step 2: Over these five minutes, simply observe yourself. What is it that you see yourself thinking and doing? Note which of these thoughts are positive, and which are negative. Remember that you're not to be in your thoughts, rather just to observe them. When you find yourself observing a negative thought that does not serve you, simply watch it pass by. When it is a constructive or positive thought, allow yourself to take special note of it, and even expand upon it.

Step 3: At the end of five minutes, reflect on which type of thoughts (negative vs. positive) you predominantly observed. Repeat this exercise often, until the positive thoughts you focus on, greatly outweigh the negative thoughts you let fly by, or they evaporate.

The more you can observe your thoughts, the more mindful you will become of only letting in what serves you. When this happens, watch how much more of the good comes into your life.

Chapter 3
EMPOWERMENT THROUGH YOUR ENVIRONMENT

"Any time you sincerely want to make a change, the first thing you must do is to raise your standards."
—Tony Robbins

What if you could enhance your energy, and improve your state of being, just by shifting your environment? You are a reflection of your surroundings. Your environment plays a big factor in how you are influenced. Your behaviors and decisions are a result of this.

Your environment and everything that you encounter every day influences your subconscious. Your subconscious dictates your consciousness. And your consciousness is where you operate most of the waking day.

Your environment either supports your growth, or hinders it. In this chapter, we are going to do an environmental audit, and go over simple ways to improve your state of being, no matter where you are.

I'm going to take you back with me to a time in my childhood when, from as early as I can remember, my mom and dad both empowered me, and immersed me in love. My dad always ended every sentence he said to me (and still does) with "sweetie girl". And my mom nurtured me with all the love she possibly could. Our home was filled with classic rock music, such as The Beatles, Stevie Ray Vaughan, Eric Clapton, and my favorite of all the music: my dad's. My dad would sing and play the guitar every single day. The words and melodies that filled our house were always uplifting and bright. My parents always made sure we ate healthy. My mom even went as far as Scotch-taping health articles to the pantry walls, so we'd always be mindful when it came to nutrition. There were also always ample outdoor activities. How I enjoyed playing outside on the grass barefoot!

HAPPINESS HABITAT

Although my family had their ups and downs, my parents made sure to shine a light on the lessons to be learned throughout any slump. When I look back, watching old home videos, it brings tears to my eyes from the joy I experienced as a child. Especially hearing how my parents spoke to me. Through this joy, I was able to be my most creative self, and my joy became contagious to others, as well.

When I grew older and moved out on my own, my environment didn't always match the same positive and supportive atmosphere that my parents had helped create for me as a child. Despite being known for my cheerful disposition, there was a time when I found myself lying to myself, and others, just to make a difficult situation seem better than it really was. This ultimately took a toll on my mental and emotional well-being.

As my joy and sense of empowerment began to fade, my environment also reflected this change. The happy, confident girl I once knew had become a distant memory; and I found myself living in fear and uncertainty. My physical health also started to deteriorate, with dull skin and brittle hair. It was only then that I realized the profound impact of my environment on my well-being. I had allowed myself to become disconnected from the supportive and positive atmosphere that had once nourished my mind, body, and spirit. How could I have let this happen?

The answer: I was not careful enough about what I let into my environment. During my early 20s, in Los Angeles, I fell into a toxic situation with an old friend. I will call him "Derek". As long as we were just friends, everything was fine. But when it evolved into relationship, for reasons I will never know, Derek did a "Dr. Jekyll/Mr. Hyde" on me. It didn't help that I fooled myself into thinking that staying with him was my only option. Many of us do this to ourselves at times. It becomes hard to know what is really going on when we are deeply *in* the situation. I was so blind to reality that I did not realize how negative my environment had become. The cheerful and bouncy Jacqlyn that I once knew was now tip-toeing on eggshells around Derek, and I had closed off access to my higher consciousness. Derek barraged me with negativity at every opportunity.

When I moved to Texas with Derek, and lived with him in his own home, yet another mean side of Derek came out that I'd never seen before. He was relentless in his efforts to tear me down, constantly telling me that I wasn't good enough. It was as though he took a sick pleasure in slamming everything I did. It could be something as simple as cutting vegetables to make dinner. He'd walk in the kitchen and start criticizing my technique with such venom that it felt like a physical blow.

On another occasion, we were on a lake, each in our own kayak. Out of the blue, Derek started screaming at me, claiming I wasn't paddling correctly. Then he furiously rowed away, abandoning me in the middle of the lake. This was particularly flabbergasting, as kayaking was second nature to me, having grown up on a lake. There were instances where he called me an idiot for reading the "wrong" book. Not a day went by that Derek didn't pile on the emotional and verbal abuse. It was dehumanizing.

One morning, I was in his bathroom when he barged in and locked the door behind him. He refused to let me leave until I agreed to sign a document he was holding. It was a deeply unsettling experience that made me realize just how trapped and vulnerable I had become in an out-of-control relationship with this dangerous man. The hostility in his eyes was so unsettling, I signed the document out of abject fear. A couple days later, when he was out of town on a business trip, I packed my bags and left. On my way back to L.A., I felt an overwhelming sense of relief wash over me. It was only then, when I had the space and the freedom to assess my situation and recognize the toxicity I had allowed into my environment, that I was able to make the necessary changes, and reclaim my joy.

HAPPINESS HABITAT

My experience serves as a powerful example of the importance of being mindful of the people and influences in our lives. It's essential to prioritize our own well-being. To take decisive steps to remove ourselves from toxic relationships. And to surround ourselves with positive and supportive people who lift us up rather than tear us down.

I was done being a victim of manipulation and verbal abuse. It was time for me to take control of my own life, and create the joy and fulfillment that I deserved. As I focused on the things that brought me happiness, and practiced self-care, I began to see a transformation in myself. The weight of the negative drama lifted. I started to feel alive again. I was no longer being held back by someone else's crazy behavior. Instead, I was able to fully embrace my own potential, and start living the life that I had always wanted. I started to grow and thrive like never before. That joyful Jacqlyn was back. It took a conscious effort to remove the toxicity, from my environment, from my life.

HAPPINESS HABITAT

Toxicity is like cancer; it starts small, then it just spreads all over, and that's what happened to me. You'd be surprised what can happen to your life when you block out the negativity, and only allow the good in. It's a feeling of freedom and abundant love. That is exactly how I have felt since then, and my self-esteem has only continued to grow.

During those months of negativity and oppression, I felt like I was living in a completely different world; one that was dark and scary. Now that I am lightyears away (metaphorically speaking of course), I can reflect on the lessons that I have since learned. As my cousin Dave likes to say, "Look for the light, love, and lessons." The biggest lesson I learned from this experience is the importance of noticing when negativity or toxic behavior is trying to invade your life. Then to remove it as soon as possible. Or in some situations, if you are not able to remove toxicity immediately, (e.g., a work environment) find your own inner positivity and make that your focus, while you steadily work toward removing yourself from the negative situation. Know your worth, raise your standards, and meet yourself there.

The next lesson, that I wish I had realized sooner, is the importance of self-love. When you truly love and prioritize yourself, it becomes automatic that you will not allow negativity or toxic behavior into your life. Life is too precious to waste on anything that does not bring peace and happiness. This experience was a clear example of how I allowed negativity to slowly creep into my environment. But there are many other factors that can also have an impact on your subconscious and overall well-being. It is important to consider the people in your life, including your friends, co-workers, and even your online interactions, or with loved ones.

It is crucial to constantly evaluate your environment, and ask yourself, "Does it support or hinder my growth?" Are the people and situations in your life uplifting and positive? Or do they bring negativity, and drain your energy?

HAPPINESS HABITAT

Everything you experience influences your subconscious. From the people you follow on social media, to the media outlets playing in the background, to the words in songs, and to the people who are around us. Take note of what is influencing you in a positive way. Reinforce those things, as they will support your expansion. Also, pay attention to the things in your life that bring you down, and hold you back. Then make a conscious effort to discard or reject them, before they establish a firm hold on you. By identifying and addressing these things, you can create space for growth and expansion in your life.

There doesn't need to be a major shift to enhance your environment. Sometimes it is the smallest changes that make the biggest difference.

Think about what you are consuming throughout your day. Do you often have the news on in the background? You might not even notice it at the time, but the negativity that is broadcasted is absolutely being absorbed by your subconscious. Do you spend a lot of time scrolling through social media? It's easy to get carried away on social media and tune into stories that aren't meaningful, and uplifting. I filter who I follow based on if that person truly inspires me with their message. It is a form of edutainment (education and entertainment). It is important to filter your environment as well as your social media. Stay inspired.

Pay attention to the conversations you have, and the words you use. Words have a powerful impact on our subconscious. The ones we hear and use regularly can shape our thoughts and beliefs. I participated in a valuable exercise at a friend's monthly group meet-up called EmpowHER. We were guided through a meditation, and asked to notice three "I am" words that came to mind. We were then instructed to set reminders in our calendars for three times a day (9 AM, 12 PM, and 5 PM) to repeat these three words to ourselves. My three words were "I am *certain*, I am *wealth*, and I am *love*." These reminders still pop up on my phone every single day since 2019, and I make a conscious effort to observe and repeat these affirmations every time. This exercise continues to be a helpful reminder of the power of words, and the importance of choosing to focus on positivity and self-love.

Since seeing and speaking these affirmations to myself, I have truly embodied the words and their meanings. My beliefs and values have become much clearer to me (certainty). I have experienced exponential manifestations of abundance in my life (wealth). Additionally, I have given and received more kindness than ever before (love). This exercise is a powerful reminder of the impact that our thoughts and words can have on our lives, and the importance of focusing on positivity and self-love.

The power of words can materialize with intent. I encourage you to try that **Exercise** for yourself. You don't have to go through a guided meditation to come up with your three words. Simply think about what you desire to bring into your life, such as love, joy, harmony, or anything else. Use your words as a magnet to attract what you desire; and make a reminder on your phone with an "I am" statement to repeat to yourself every day. For example, if you desire to be in a relationship in the near future, experiment with saying "I am love" every day and observe what happens. Remember that frequency attracts like frequency. By focusing on positivity and self-love, you can bring these same things into your life.

In addition to auditing your environment, and practicing self-love, it's also important to have the tools to manage your emotions and navigate difficult situations. When life gets tough, it can be challenging to get yourself out of a negative or stressful environment. That's where people like **Dr. Carolyn Daitch** come in. She is an internationally renowned psychologist with expertise in anxiety, stress, and emotion management. This incredible woman also happens to be my cousin. Dr. Carolyn Daitch has helped thousands of people, and I have been lucky enough to be one of them. I had the opportunity to speak with her in the summer of 2020, to discuss her strategies for managing stress and anxiety. These can be especially useful when your environment negatively impacts you. By having the right tools and resources for stress and anxiety, you can better equip yourself to handle difficult situations, and maintain your well-being.

> **Jacqlyn:** Thank you so much for joining me today. I would love to begin this conversation at the fundamental level. What is anxiety?
>
> **Carolyn:** Well, anxiety is kind of a combination of fear and stress. And about 20% of us are born that way. About 20% of babies have anxiety. Right from the get-go, they're temperamentally primed to be overreactive to stressors. These little babies tend to be anxious kids, and anxious adolescents, and anxious adults. Now, having said that, the rest of us who may or may not have

anxiety by nature are becoming anxious during this pandemic. It's worse for people who are vulnerable to it. But, it's also not easy, even for those of us who don't have that anxious temperament.

Jacqlyn: Okay. You're born with it, or you can develop it. I'm curious. If you are born with it, how do you go through life? This is kind of a two-part question. How do you go throughout life being able to manage those emotions? I guess we can start there, because more than likely, people might have anxiety, and they don't know what to do with it.

Carolyn: First of all, one of the things that I teach is for people to catch it. I mean, we can walk around with our bodies feeling stressed. And unless we're overwhelmingly stressed, like we're having a panic attack or pain in our gut, we may not even catch it. It's like walking around with a mild temperature. You don't know you're sick. But you're just a little bit sick. I have people first try to scan their bodies, scan their minds, scan their feelings, so that we can catch it before there's a tsunami. In other words, it's easy to manage a little bit of a flood. But if it is a tsunami, we just have to roll with it till it's over. We may or may not know. Again, people with overwhelming panic disorder or severe OCD, which is obsessive-compulsive disorder, they know it. But for the more subtle kinds of things, you have to train yourself to kind of observe. Not obsess, but just kind of observe.

Jacqlyn: I find myself observing myself all the time. How do you get your mind around observing if you're already in that anxiety state? I've encountered people who have this issue where they know they have anxiety. Or they know they have mild

OCD, and they're not really sure what to do about it. It just happens, and they can't control it.

Carolyn: The first thing you do is label it. You say, "There's the worry..." I'll give one for me. I have a lot on my plate right now. So, I might say, "There's the worry: I won't get it all done." Then I imagine that I'm putting it five feet in front of me. It's not like *I'm* worried. Note the words: "There's the worry." We're not fused with it. There it is, just like there is the lake, or there is my mother, or there it is. Just be with it. Paradoxically, we do want to be with it for a little bit. When I first started doing therapy, and even now, people would come in and say, "Dr. Daitch, I want to get rid of my anxiety. I just want to get rid of it!" What I've learned over the years is that we don't get rid of it, we *manage* it. The first step of managing is just noticing it, then labeling it. What I like to do, the model that I teach, is that once you catch it, then you self-soothe. Because you cannot listen to your own objective wise thoughts. Or your friend's wise thoughts. Or your therapist's wise thoughts ... until you're in a state of calm.

Jacqlyn, I know you're not a worrier. But, let's say you were worried about, I don't know, whether or not you're going to get sick with coronavirus on the plane back to California. Your friends will say, "Jacqlyn, it's a risk. But you'll wear a mask, and you're young, and you'll make sure there's no one in the middle seat." However, if you're in an anxious state, revved up – what we call a sympathetic nervous system – where you're just really anxious, you won't hear me saying, "Jacqlyn, you'll probably be okay." You'll hear it maybe in a whisper (lowers her voice), "You'll be okay." But you'll be saying, "No, I won't!" Until you chill down the part of our brain... We call it the amygdala, it's in our emotional brain. Until we chill that down, we can't listen to our neocortex, which is reasonable.

What I think makes my work a bit unique – and it's different than standard cognitive behavioral therapy, which is very popular – is this: I really believe that we need to, first of all, be mindful and accepting of our feelings, and then moving to calm. That's where I use hypnosis, or any other calming techniques, like breathing, or tensing and relaxing, or yoga. We need to move into quiet, and it takes a few minutes. Then you can be rational. Then you can say, "What is the likelihood that this is going to happen?" Then you can say, "Possibilities are not probabilities. It is possible to be in a plane crash, but it's not probable."

Jacqlyn: Wow! And what about for the other person involved in the engagement: For a spouse, son, daughter, niece, nephew? In the action where the other person is actually having a panic attack, an anxiety attack, acting very irrational, and that person can see, "Okay, clearly something's going on." What is the best way the help this person?

Carolyn: I wrote a whole book to answer this question. My third book is called *Anxious in Love*. It's about what it is like to be in a relationship with somebody who's anxious. Or, if you're anxious to be in a relationship with somebody who's not anxious. And what people do naturally, you shouldn't do. What people do naturally is, they try to talk somebody out of their panic. They say, "You have no reason to be this upset. You're okay. You're fine. If you get sick, we'll get you help." Like in the example I gave for fear of flying, which is really common, it's to say, "I can't believe, Jacqlyn, you're afraid of flying. You know it's more dangerous to drive to the airport. You drive on the freeway in California every day. That's so much more dangerous than flying on a plane. You are a reasonable woman. Why would you be so scared?" Never start that way because when an anxious person is panicking, their emotional brain is taking charge.

As I pointed out in my book called *Lost in Translation*, you are communicating to a part of the brain that can't hear you. What you do instead is you say, "I know you're scared. I understand. It makes sense that you're scared. You are scared because you know somebody who was in a plane crash, or you heard on TV somebody had a plane crash. It's got to be really awful to be that scared." Usually, the other person then calms down because they feel heard, and not judged.

Then you ask permission. You say, "Are you open to hearing my perspective?" You could say, "Remember what Dr. Daitch told you. That when you're having a panic attack, you can just ride through it. Or you can move ahead in time when it is over." I like this one: You can also put frozen oranges on your cheeks to abort a panic attack. "Remember Dr. Daitch told you about that," if they're in therapy. Or, "Let's go for a walk."

Jacqlyn: That's incredible. Even an orange can help...

Carolyn: It doesn't have to be an orange, but it kind of fits your fit.

Jacqlyn: Cool!

Carolyn: It's very cool. So, whatever it is, you start with empathizing, not reasoning. That's why I try to bring every spouse, or sometimes daughter or son, into a session at least once. Because, the well-meaning family member will always start with trying to reason. Indeed, I'll be a little parenthetical. Here in Detroit, where I'm from, many, many anxious people are married to engineers. We're in the car business. There's a lot of engineers around. Maybe I'm being a bit "sexist", but anxiety here is more common in women. Three to one. They'll be drawn to their engineer boyfriend because he can fix *everything*. He's chilled. He's reasonable. But when they get married, and she is anxious, even the nicest guy will say – again, it could be the reverse – "You really shouldn't be anxious, dear. Everything is fine here. You don't have lung cancer. You just have a cold. You know that."

But the woman with anxiety feels misunderstood, a little judged. What happens next is they get angry at each other – this is explained in that book – then they retreat like it's helpless: "I can't reason with this woman!" "He doesn't understand me!" "He doesn't care about me!" "He thinks I'm an idiot!" That's why we start with empathy. Very few people know that because if we're not scared, we start with our own reason. Does that make sense to you?

Jacqlyn: Yes, absolutely. I want to jump back to that person who is working on overcoming their anxiety, or working through it. You said it is in part to do with the stress as well.

Carolyn: Yes.

Jacqlyn: In daily life, working a nine-to-five, or working for yourself, whatever you're doing in life, how do you deal with that in the everyday occurrences you have, to keep you in high peak performance? Because, I think at the higher levels of life, there can be higher perceived stress.

Carolyn: Right.

Jacqlyn: How do you handle that? How do you manage that stress?

Carolyn: What I recommend people do – and this is in the last book, *Road to Calm Workbook* – is every day to practice what I call "stress inoculation". What that means is, every day for about twenty minutes, you move into calm. I have an app for that, and I have a recording. But it doesn't have to be mine. If you're a meditator, meditate for twenty minutes. Or, you could do yoga and meditation for twenty minutes. There are countless apps now available. So, for twenty minutes, just see if you can start the day with calm, okay?

Jacqlyn: Beautiful! What is your app called again?

Carolyn: It's called the "Road to Calm Companion".

Jacqlyn: That's amazing!

Carolyn: In that book, there is also a link to an audio recording that people who are techie can... I mean, when I first created it, people still had CD players. Now, they're getting to be all integrated. You can download it to your phone. Then, throughout the day, take two minutes to simply do one of the techniques I teach.

Again, there's the time urgency. For me, it's often. There it is. There's the time urgency. Breathe through it. Breathe for two minutes. That's all you need. And if you could do it five times a day, it will be terrific.

Actually, to be honest, I get most of my clients to do the morning one. But then, they forget that during the day. They're on go, go, go. So then, you link it in. Like, for physicians, I'll say, "Every couple hours, before you open the door to the next patient, do your two minutes." Or with you, before you go on to your next project,

Jacqlyn, take two minutes. It's hard to remember because we get on one speed. I get on one speed and that's "Go!"

Jacqlyn: I can relate!

Carolyn: We have to remember to do that. During those two minutes, we can do some self-hypnosis, too. Like, if I were doing two minutes — for me, I've got a lot of projects right now — in those two minutes, I can say, "There's the time urgency, but you always get it done." That's the truth. I always get it done.

Jacqlyn: You're almost hypnotizing yourself?

Carolyn: Yes, right. You can do that at the end of the twenty minutes in the morning, or throughout the day, catching your fears. I've been using a metaphor recently. It's in the course. I love it. And it's not original to me. I don't know who developed it first, so I can't give an exact credit for it. It's a cognitive-behavioral technique. But I combined it with hypnosis, where you imagine a courtroom, okay? You just close your eyes and see the wood, and the green carpeting, and the judge in the robe. Imagine there are two attorneys. One is the defense attorney. The defense attorney is defending your fears: "Yes, it really is dangerous to go on a plane. People are dying of the coronavirus, and blah, blah, blah, blah, blah. Maybe, somebody isn't wearing a mask. It's unreasonable to fly for years till there's an effective vaccine."

Then, there's a prosecuting attorney who gets the other position that says, "Well, there is a risk, but the reality is that you're taking Delta, and they're not selling middle seats. The reality is, you're wearing a mask, and now they're mandating masks. The reality is, you're washing your hands, and you're taking food on the plane, and you're trying not to drink, so you don't need to go to the bathroom. You're wiping off your seats, and you're wiping everything off, and they've wiped it off. There is some risk, but not as risky as you say." That's the prosecuting attorney.

Then, you close your eyes and you see the judge. Imagine a judge wearing his or her black robe. The judge represents the wisest part of you, the part of you that is intelligent and calm and has had a lifetime of experiences. Maybe not the experience that we're in right now, but a lot of challenges. From your own wise judge, why don't you make a verdict right now? What would you give as a verdict if you were a judge for that fear? What would you do, Jacqlyn? What would you say as your own wise judge right now?

Jacqlyn: I would probably say, "Everything is going to be okay. Take proper precaution. Collect data, and move forward. And do not live in fear. Live in certainty of your health, and that everything is going to be okay.

Carolyn: Right.

Jacqlyn: You believe you'll be okay.

Carolyn: Yes. Or, even if you're not okay, it'll *be* okay. This is a unique situation (the Pandemic) because some people will die, but most of the time it will be okay.

Jacqlyn: I want to touch on mindfulness while going throughout the day, managing your emotions. Because I know you specialize in this as well. How can you stay in this flow state with all the distractions in the outside world? I know when I am in flow, I am also on center, or balance, you could say. What happens when you fall off that center, and you need to get back there?

Carolyn: I was telling a patient this morning, "It's a lifelong process." I mean, it's one thing if you're a Buddhist monk living in some kind of ashram. And even they, I'm sure, get off balance. I'm sure they do. But they have so much support for being in mindfulness. For somebody like myself, it's an ongoing struggle. But the way we can do it – and I'm sure you're aware of some of these things – first of all, just catching your breathing. Just being with your breathing, mindful walking, that being really not power walking. Rather, noticing the trees, noticing the sounds, noticing what your feet feel like on the ground. That can be a mindfulness exercise. Even a simple one that I gave my client this morning. I said... I'll do this with you. Stand up.

Jacqlyn: Okay.

HAPPINESS HABITAT

Carolyn: And just say to yourself, "I'm standing."

Jacqlyn: I'm standing.

Carolyn: Just be aware of standing. Notice your breathing as you stand. Then, sit down. And just think. You don't even have to say, "I'm sitting." So, all day long, we are standing and sitting. Just commenting on it moves you into mindfulness. Or, "I'm tasting that ice cream. And it's really sweet." If you get in a mindful... Probably not for you because you are so nice and thin. But for most of us, we'll eat a whole bowl of ice cream and we don't even taste it. We taste the first couple of spoonfuls. But then, we just eat it mindlessly. But if we're in *mindfulness,* and we taste how sweet and cold it is, we may not need to eat the whole bowl. And so it is, all day long.

We have opportunities. For me, one of the huge annoyances of life is being on hold on the phone. They'll say, "We appreciate your patience," and I get so mad. I am not patient at all. What do you mean I'm patient? That can be a time for you to go, "Oh, there's the annoyance of being put on hold. What can I do while I'm on hold? I can simply breathe."

Jacqlyn: I find those moments too as an opportunity to challenge myself to go into a state of calm.

Carolyn: Exactly.

Jacqlyn: I'm curious to know, too, what are your views on happiness? I want to know what happiness means to you. And where do you think happiness plays a part in our everyday life, as a productive and optimized human?

Carolyn: Well, I'm going to flip the question around and say, "How do you treat depression?" if that's okay.

Jacqlyn: Totally.

Carolyn: When people are depressed, there are things they can do to get them happier and out of depression. But they don't want to do them because ... you're in a depressed state, you kind of are in a "Why bother?" state. Like nothing's going to help. The first thing they have to do – I shouldn't say first, but it's pretty high up there – is to *move*. Walk, move. They will say, "I just don't want to get out of bed." Move, even if it's just down the street. Actually, there has been research that exercise is almost as effective as antidepressants for depression and anxiety. Antidepressants are just a smidgen more effective, but not much. Not much at all. Simply exercise. I'd like people to exercise daily, not three times a week. Daily. Even if they exercise for fifteen minutes, ten minutes.

The next thing when we're depressed, we withdraw. We don't want to talk to people. So, I push people to get on the phone and call people, or text people, or text by SMS. I'm much older than you, and I'm not in a world where everything is texting. I mean, what happened to a voice on the other end of the phone?

Jacqlyn: I love FaceTiming. This is my favorite type of digital interaction.

Carolyn: Yes. And Zooming, because we need to connect to other people. We are not meant to be islands. Next, we need to accomplish things. I tell people, "Just clean out one drawer. Throw away the old food in the refrigerator. Return those emails." It's movement and connection and accomplishment to get you out of depression. Now, people can start on the road to happiness. It is not a switch if you're depressed. If they do those things, they will feel better.

HAPPINESS HABITAT

Then, what I do with people has to do with their orientation in time. If you're anxious, you have a distorted sense of time. You live in the future ... what can go wrong in the future? If you're depressed, you think about everything that went wrong in the past: "I shouldn't have broken up with that guy." "I should have gotten a master's degree and not stop there." "I should have moved to San Francisco instead of La Jolla." Whatever it is. They are our regrets, or all those things we leave in the past. With people who are sad, I have them go into the future when they are feeling better. I'll just talk about how all feelings are transient. So, go into future time... Like I said with the Pandemic, go into the future. I will do it with people with anxiety, have them go into a positive future, not a scary future. That's one of the hypnotic techniques I use.

Jacqlyn: When you're in an anxiety state of mind, you tend to be looking into the future and you might have a million things on your plate. How do you find that perfect balance?

Carolyn: You keep working on it every day. And again, a lot of people with anxiety are not productive because they get paralyzed.

Jacqlyn: Got it.

Carolyn: A student who's really anxious about their college essay will find they can't write a word. Or somebody who badly wants a job, gets so anxious about it, they cancel the interview because they are afraid. Anxiety isn't necessarily correlated with productivity. It's probably a little confusing because I wanted to have enough worry to do a good job. But if I were really, really anxious, I wouldn't be with you right now. I'd be too worried that either I wouldn't look good, or I wouldn't sound good, or whatever it is. How do you do that? You keep reining back. You keep moving back into balance. For myself, am I trying to do too much today? Yeah? Rein it back.

This afternoon, I'm going to go swimming and not do any productive work. For somebody who's avoiding doing their college essays, or their housework, they need to push themselves. We're always trying to... even the balance scale. Maybe some of us are just naturally balanced. But most people are not. It's not easy. It requires a lot of work. I wish I had been like you at your age.

Jacqlyn: I've been learning from you from a young age. I'm so grateful.

Carolyn: Thank you, Jacqlyn.

Having the tools to manage your emotions, and the knowledge and skills to carefully evaluate your environment, are essential components of creating your Happiness Habitat. When you are able to manage your emotions, and surround yourself with positive and supportive people and situations, you Optimize Your Opportunity Zone.

EXERCISE 4

Take as much time as is needed to carefully evaluate your environment. Think about the people and things that fill your space most of the time. Make a list of everything that comes to mind. Once you have this list, take some time to consider which elements of your environment empower you, and which ones diminish your well-being. Circle the items on your list that bring you joy and fulfillment, and cross out the ones that negatively impact you. If you're unsure about certain items on your list, take the time to explore your feelings and come to a decision.

Once you've completed this process, it's time to take action. Consider removing or limiting exposure to anything that isn't uplifting or supportive. For example, if you follow people on social media who

HAPPINESS HABITAT

consistently post negative or triggering content, consider unfollowing or muting them. The same goes for music, or other forms of media, that convey a negative message, or bring you down. As another example, does the music you listen to constantly talk down, or convey a message that isn't uplifting? I know this may seem extreme, but cut it down. Or even cut it out. Everything influences your subconscious.

On the other hand, use the circled items on this list as a guide to incorporate more of the things that bring you joy and fulfillment. Remember that everything we consume has an impact on our subconscious; so it's important to be mindful of what we allow into our environment. This exercise is meant to help you create a Happiness Habitat that supports your growth and well-being. Please enjoy the process, and make it meaningful.

Write a reflection on this exercise, including any insights or observations you gained from the process. What did you learn about your environment and how it impacts

HAPPINESS HABITAT

your well-being? What changes did you make? And how did those changes affect your happiness and sense of fulfillment?

Chapter 4
ORGANIZE AND ENHANCE YOUR SPACE

"Now imagine yourself living in a space that contains only things that spark joy. Isn't this the lifestyle you dream of?"
—*Marie Kondo*

In this chapter I am going to share my best organization and environment hacks to enhance your Happiness Habitat.

Now that you have audited your environment for anything that does not empower you, it's time to organize and build in your space, to enhance your empowerment and clarity.

Have you ever walked into a room and felt at home and warm? On the other hand, have you ever walked into a room that felt unwelcoming and cold? Imagine an old doctor's office with scratchy fabric chairs placed everywhere, bright lighting, and slightly crooked art hanging on the wall. Does this cold room sound inviting to you?

Probably not. Now, let's switch it up. Imagine walking into a warm living room where there is symmetry in the placement of the chairs. Books are neatly arranged. And the room is filled with the soothing aroma of vanilla candles. Which room would you rather be in? I'm sure it's the warm room! Let's dive into the understanding of this, and how you can create a warm, welcoming, and productive environment.

When I was growing up, my mom and dad would always make sure the house was organized and tidy. From labeled containers, to perfectly placed furniture, to uncluttered surfaces, it all just made sense. There was also an amazing ambiance that I remember very well; my emotions were flooded with bliss. My dad had his guitars nicely placed around the main room, with his blue neon guitar perfectly positioned in the corner. An immaculate ambiance that lit up the tall ceilings and reflected against the white walls and stone fireplace. My clothes either had to be in the hamper or neatly folded. The food in our fridge was always organized, and put in their respective locations, with the labels always front facing. My dad kept his tool shop symmetrical and organized. Because of this, he always knew where every single tool was at all times. His home office was always tidy and free of loose papers. Even when my mom set the table, the placemats were aligned with the forks and napkins in perfect symmetry.

    I have brought this same practice into my adult life, in my office, my home, and any other space where I can make a difference. When I was staying with my cousins during the earlier months of the Pandemic, sometimes I'd visit their pantry room. The clutter would always prevent me from easily finding what I was looking for. There'd be open bags of chips all over, and multiples of the same cans in different locations. Finally, toward the later end of my stay, my cousins gave me the green light to completely reorganize their pantry. My younger cousin and I completely tore the room up, positively of course. We actually had a blast doing this together and I was glad for the opportunity. When the rest of the family checked out the pantry and saw the "remodel" they could not stop gushing on how much more open and free they felt (physically and mentally).

A welcoming environment is a space where you feel comfortable and at ease. Therefore, your productivity is more likely to remain in flow. Have you ever found yourself standing in front of an open fridge, unsure of what to grab, even though you've opened it five times in a row? When the fridge is organized and clean, you never have to hesitate. Everyone operates best in their own way; so I'm not here to dictate any one way to be most efficient in your space. However, I will share with you my best practices for empowering your space and you, to optimizing flow and efficiency in your physical spaces:

- Keep each activity to its respected environment. What does this mean? For example, if you sleep in your room, don't also eat and work in the same place. By keeping your bed solely for sleeping, you are more likely to fall asleep faster, because your brain associates the bed with sleep.

- If you have roommates or live in a small space, it is important to keep activities and their areas distinct from one another. This will help you optimize each activity, and create neural pathways that allow you to jump into the flow of these activities much quicker.

- If you work from home and tend to work at your kitchen table, you may find yourself snacking more than usual. Sometimes, all you have to do is make a mental shift. But I personally find that creating physical separation between activities can help improve your flow. For example, if you usually sit in the same seat at the dining table to work, try sitting in a different seat.

- Take note of how you operate best in each environment, and if you want to improve your flow in any area, ask yourself if you're "double-dipping" any activities in the same places.

- If you want to improve your ability to quickly enter a state of flow for various activities, try creating a dedicated space for each activity. This can help prevent distractions and improve your focus and productivity. For example, many of my friends have a dedicated space in their home where they journal. This helps them quickly enter a state of flow and optimize their time.

Let's go deeper...

- In each of these respective environments, what does it look like? Is there clutter? Can anything be better organized to be more visually appealing? Your outer world is a reflection of your inner world. It is harder to feel anxious in an organized environment than it is in a cluttered environment. It's important to remain open here, as it can be easy to leave a "mess" just because you think you are efficient in a cluttered environment. What if I told you that you could increase your production just by cleaning up? "In 2011, researchers at Princeton University found that clutter can actually make it more difficult to focus on a particular task. Specifically, they found that the visual cortex can be overwhelmed by task-irrelevant objects, making it harder to allocate attention and complete tasks efficiently." (psychologytoday.com).

- Take time to organize and straighten up your environment. If there are books lying around in many different areas, flip them around to all show the same way, and put them in one spot. Personally, I organize my books by color in my home office, which is beautiful to look at, and makes it easy for my brain to identify which book I'm looking for. But hey, if you find it more visually appealing to organize your books another way, then do it!

- If there are chairs in your space that are misaligned, be sure to align them.

- Another organizing hack, specifically for storage areas, is to contain items by category in clear labeled bins. My whole art area (which you'd think should be messy) is organized in clear containers so I can easily find anything quickly. There is nothing like being in the middle of a painting and knowing exactly where to find the mellow yellow colored acrylic paint.

- One of my favorite organizing hacks for cooking is the order of my spice drawer. I organize my spices alphabetically, which saves me a lot of time while I am in the flow of making a dish. Listening to your intuition and finding what brings you joy can be a great way to improve your organizational skills, and enhance your living environment.

Marie Kondo is a master organizer. Her techniques have helped me learn a lot

HAPPINESS HABITAT

about creating a tidy home. I reached out to her team to learn more about the importance of this practice. According to them, a clean and organized space can have a positive impact on your overall well-being and happiness. Here is what the team shared with me from Marie:

> "Many people have equated my tidying method with minimalism, but it's quite different. Minimalism advocates living with less; the KonMari Method™ encourages living among items you truly cherish."

> "The first step in my tidying method is to imagine your ideal lifestyle. For some, this vision might be to surround yourself with the bare essentials. For others, it could mean living in a home teeming with beloved art, books, collections, and heirlooms."

> "Joy is personal. Each individual's ideal life – and space – will look different from the next. If minimalism is a lifestyle that sparks joy for

someone, I encourage that. In the same way, if someone has determined that many items in their life spark joy, that's okay, too!"

"Clutter obscures what's most important. Discarding that which does not support your ideal lifestyle; that creates space for treasured possessions to truly shine; and leaves room for future joy-sparking additions. One of the reasons I suggest packing lightly is to make sure you can bring back joy-sparking souvenirs from your travels – as long as you have room for it back home."

Take some time to reflect on what sparks joy for you, and use that to guide your efforts to declutter and organize your home.

Keeping each environment to its respective activity, and adding clarity and organization to your environment, are just a few ways you can optimize your space. Now, let's explore adding the finishing touches.

HAPPINESS HABITAT

Scents and living organisms are a great way to produce joy in a space. Simply adding soy candles, or clean diffusers, for example, can help make your zone feel warmer. Adding living plants will also aid in the warmth of your environment. A study done by Green Life Industry showed a group of people who had plants in their awareness found reductions in stress levels and negative feelings of a magnitude of 30-60% over a three month test.

A welcoming space is one that is clean, organized, and promotes a sense of harmony. Create the room for unhindered growth. I love creating the best possible experience in my environment; it enhances my flow and joy. From my diffusers, to my eucalyptus shower spray, to the inspiring art on my walls... it is important to build spaces for yourself that feel clear and connected. By adding small touches to your environment, you can create a joyful experience that will make a lasting impact.

EXERCISE 5

Now, it's time to audit your environment and optimize it for optimal efficiency and joy. Even if you already feel your home is tidy and spotless, still take a moment to go deeper. There's always room for improvement.

1. Begin by conducting an audit of your environment, room by room. Take note of any areas that are cluttered or disorganized. Then make a plan to address those issues. This can help to create a more peaceful and harmonious atmosphere in your home.

2. As you audit your environment, also think about how you can optimize each activity in that space. For example, if you spend a lot of time in your home office, you might want to think about how you can improve the lighting, layout, or ergonomics of that space to make it more comfortable and efficient.

HAPPINESS HABITAT

3. Once you have completed your initial audit, make a plan to regularly review and improve your spaces. Set aside time each month to go through your rooms and see what can be improved. This will help you to stay on top of clutter, and make sure that your environment is always conducive to productivity and happiness.

4. As you work to improve your environment, remember to keep each activity in its respective environment. For example, if you sleep in your bedroom, try to avoid eating and working in that space. This can help you to optimize each activity and create neural pathways that allow you to jump into the flow of activities more quickly.

5. Finally, don't be afraid to experiment and try new things to make your environment even better. Whether it is adding a new plant to your living room, rearranging your furniture, or

simply adding in diffusers, small changes can make a big difference in creating a joyful and welcoming space.

Chapter 5
WHAT YOU CONSUME, CONSUMES YOU

"The food you eat can be either the safest and most powerful form of medicine, or the slowest form of poison." —Ann Wigmore

In the "Raising Your Vibration" chapter, I shared what happens when your body is under chronic stress: It is focused on removing that perceived stress, leaving no room for other things to grow or expand. Without a foundation for success, you rule out the opportunity to perform and operate at your highest potential. It's easy to operate as a superhuman if you have the same knowledge and data as one.

I've been seriously studying health and wellness since the age of 14. In the home where I grew up, my environment was also one of health and wellness. My mom, an intensive care nurse, always studied best health practices. She even had health facts and nutrition information posted on the pantry shelves.

    This emphasis on mindful consumption goes back to my dad's mom, who was known as "Mrs. Atkins" to my dad's childhood friends. She served mainly high-protein, green meals, with few carbs. As a result, my dad was instilled with the importance of mindful consumption, which was then passed down to me. Our house always had vegetable-rich meals. It was not the "fun" snack house, because it was filled with non-processed foods, and lots of fruits and veggies. While it may not have been popular with my childhood friends at the time, I am grateful for this now. My subconscious was filled with health-minded data from an early age, which led to my conscious decision to study health and wellness on my own. From books to documentaries to case studies, I filled my brain with knowledge about optimizing my mind and body.

My "why" had also expanded beyond me. It stemmed from wanting to improve the life of one of my relatives. When my cousin (who I shall call "Daniel" to protect his privacy) became ill, and was put on several heavy medications in an attempt to combat the symptoms of his disease, the doctor did not audit Daniel's diet. I took it upon myself to learn more about how food consumption affects the body. Although Daniel already had a moderately good diet and fitness regimen, and even had an allergy test done, I still saw an opportunity for improvement. I remember Daniel telling me, "During a doctor's visit, I was told my liver enzymes were too high, and he wanted to increase the dosage on one of my medications."

I cared too much to just let this happen. The drug's side effects were already troublesome for him. Although I wasn't a doctor, I knew that if food wasn't being looked at as a factor, I could potentially aid in support here. With his consent, I stepped in and worked with Daniel, cutting out certain foods to counteract his chronic disease. After all, humans consume food multiple times a day, so it's important to be aware of everything you are putting in your body. A week later, after cutting out dairy and certain high lectin foods, when Daniel went in for his next liver enzymes test, it had come down to near normal level. The doctor discounted the diet shift; he said it must have been a coincidence. Although this doctor was well-respected, Daniel told me that he knew it was the combination of the diet change, along with the all-natural vitamins I suggested, that led to his improved liver enzyme levels. As a result, his disease was now more manageable.

I am always deeply immersed in studying health and wellness. If I'm putting something in my body, my rule of thumb is that it must serve me positively, and be an asset to my overall health and well-being.

Whatever you consume has an impact on you. Your overall health and wellness practices directly affect your ability to perform at your best. In other words, to run like a Ferrari, you must fuel yourself like one. If you want to perform at optimum level, you must first understand how food reacts in the body. Suffice to say, not all food is created equal. You owe it to yourself to understand the value, negative or positive, of food so you can be more mindful with your choices. It is also important to understand the human body's relationship with food on an organ level. Many nutritionists say that your gut is your second brain. Your gut communicates with the rest of your body, so taking care of it is essential.

The gut microbiome plays a crucial role in communicating with the body's immune system. As mentioned previously, when your body is not under stress, it can focus on expanding and growing, rather than contracting and defending. You only get to experience this lifetime once, so why not make it the best experience you can possibly have? Everyone's path to optimal health is different, but understanding how to improve your gut and overall health will be beneficial for maximizing the optimization of your life.

HAPPINESS HABITAT

Scientific research has shown that the gut microbiome plays a significant role in many aspects of health, including digestion, immunity, mental health, and even heart health. By supporting the health of your gut microbiome, you can improve your overall well-being and quality of life.

After reading Dr. Steven Gundry's book, *The Plant Paradox*, I became much more mindful about my food choices. It was simple yet incredibly impactful. Dr. Steven Gundry is a well-renowned cardiologist, heart surgeon, medical researcher, and author. His mission is to improve health, happiness, and longevity through a unique vision of human nutrition. In the beginning of his book, he talks about the evolution of plants. Just like humans have evolved over time, plants too have evolved; and it was fascinating to learn about the symbiosis between the two. This story greatly impacted me, and I will share with you what I believe to be relative to becoming more mindful about your food choices.

HAPPINESS HABITAT

Imagine a world where the only thing that existed on this planet were plants. In this world, plants never had to worry about getting stepped on or eaten. There was no threat to their existence. Then, imagine some thousands of years later, dinosaurs emerged and began eating these plants. Just like that, the plants' world changed. Plants had to create defense mechanisms in order to survive.

Plants are aware of their purpose to reproduce. They know that they will eventually be eaten, so they let the predator know when they are ready to be devoured. Simple cues, such as color, are helpful in letting the animal or insect know when it is time to be eaten. For example, think of a banana. When it is green, it is not ripe enough; but when it turns yellow, it is ready to be eaten.

What is this defense mechanism that plants use? A plant will produce lectins in order to irritate or kill whatever tries to eat it before it is ready to pass on its offspring.

Lectins are a type of protein, and when an insect, for example, tries to eat a vegetable that is high in lectins (meaning it is not yet ready to be eaten), the insect will intake the lectins as poison, killing or severely irritating the insect.

When humans eat plants that are high in lectins, we might experience a stomach ache, runny nose, or some other type of discomfort. Although there are some use cases where we humans will bare the ache to enjoy the vegetable. Think of the last time you ate something extra spicy. You probably got a runny nose. This is actually a result of eating a large quantity of lectins.

I am going to delve deeper into understanding the interaction of lectins with the human body and its potential applications. When lectins enter the body, they bind to carbohydrates and sugars, disrupting cellular communication and causing inflammation. These lectins are capable of mimicking the cells in the gut, resulting in toxicity. Even individuals with less sensitive gut systems are affected by lectins. By removing lectin stressors, we can redirect the body's energy to other processes. In general, lectin-rich foods are unripe seeded fruits and vegetables. "The highest concentrations of the most potent plant lectins are found in the seeds, roots, young shoots, and bark of plants. In seeds, lectins are primarily found in the bran-rich outer coating, which is one reason why even whole grains are not necessarily healthy." (Diagnosis Diet). To consume high-lectin foods like beans safely, it is important to cook them thoroughly to inactivate the lectins. To learn more about lectins and their effects on the gut, consider reading *The Plant Paradox* or conducting research online.

Here are a few ways to reduce your lectin intake: Eat fruits and vegetables when they are ripe. Lightly cook your seeded vegetables, and avoid eating the seeds. Lectins are found in all plants, but raw legumes and whole grains have the highest amounts. You can reduce lectins in legumes by soaking them in water and thoroughly cooking them.

Now let's explore the other sources of protein where lectins can be found: Fish and land animals. As you may know, most animal protein you eat is just recycled protein. For example, when you eat beef, you are also consuming what the cow ate: plants. Be mindful of what you put in your body and its source. When you eat animal or fish protein, you may also be consuming recycled lectins. If the animals or fish eat a lot of lectins, then you are too. Many cows, for example, are fed corn, which is full of lectins. The meat industry often fattens animals for consumption, and lectins can do this for animals. To best avoid lectins in land animals, look for meat that is grass-fed.

Eating a low-processed, high-wholesome, plant-based diet can help reduce stressors in the body. I have adopted a natural diet, and I avoid processed, packaged foods that often contain artificial preservatives, dyes, or chemicals. Consider the difference between vegetables left out on the kitchen counter for a few weeks, and a bag of potato chips left out for the same time. While the chips may last longer, they also contain chemicals and preservatives that enter your body. Depending on the type of preservative, excess consumption of them can weaken heart tissue and cause negative health effects. Can you imagine if the FDA required food labels to list preservative side effects? The more wholesome foods you consume, the easier it is for your body to digest, and the less you have to worry about creating short-term or long-term health issues. If possible, opt for organic produce as the nonorganic variety is often sprayed with toxic chemicals to protect against insects. Remember, you are what you eat. Treat your body like a premium car and it will continue to run smoothly. As the saying goes, "health is wealth," so just as you count your money, make sure you're taking count of what you're consuming.

    I also take vitamins that are naturally sourced to help maintain my immune system and overall health. My favorite vitamins are MaryRuth Organics liquid multivitamins. These vitamins are non-GMO, plant-based, created with vegan ingredients, have the fewest allergens possible, and are sourced with the highest-quality ingredients. Many people do not know that some vitamins are created synthetically; and they can actually affect the body adversely. I also prefer liquid vitamins because they are more bioavailable than capsules. Studies show that liquid vitamins have a 98% absorption rate, while capsules only have a 3% absorption rate. When the body takes capsules, it rushes to break down the barrier, and nutrients can be lost during digestion.

    I interviewed **MaryRuth Ghiyam**, the founder of MaryRuth Organics, to get her take on the importance of nutrition. MaryRuth has been an inspiration to me since 2016, as her work has greatly influenced my understanding of the health and wellness sphere. A passionate health enthusiast, wellness advocate, and entrepreneur, MaryRuth is devoted to helping individuals lead healthier, more fulfilling lives. She remains steadfast in her mission to inspire and empower others to take control of their own well-being. I'm so grateful to have had the pleasure to interview her on my podcast, and I am thrilled to share our enlightening conversation with you, here:

> **Jacqlyn:** Thank you so much for joining me today. Let's dive right into it. Tell me about MaryRuth Organics.
>
> **MaryRuth:** Okay. I think the most beautiful part about our product line is actually how it came to be. In New York City, I had a private practice on Forty-Seventh and Third. This was before we even made the products. I saw clients in my office starting around 2013. Everyone was a very busy, career-oriented professional, who didn't have a lot of time. So, a concept that I taught them was "liquids till lunch". It was drinking tea, coffee, green juice, or smoothies until lunchtime. It is basically for more

energy. So, when everyone was doing liquids till lunch, they'd complain that when they took capsules or pills, they were very nauseous and uncomfortable. They didn't want to take their vitamins and drink liquids till lunch. That's where I got the idea to make a liquid multivitamin full spectrum.

Right now, we have over 60 products. They are all non-GMO, gluten-free, vegan. What's interesting is, out of the 60 products, the first one that we ever made is still our number one bestseller. It is the liquid morning raspberry vitamin, and its full spectrum has everything that someone would need if they are getting their bloodwork done. Obviously, they should check with their doctor. But liquids are 98% bioavailable and absorbable. Whereas pills and capsules are only like 3% to 21%. I really have seen through all of our customers' testimonials and emails –

we get hundreds and hundreds of emails a day – when people were deficient in something, taking our products really did improve their health, their energy, and the quality of their life.

Jacqlyn: I absolutely love your products. I've been taking them for years and I feel amazing. And I definitely spread the word, because it's such an important thing to actually take the most utmost healthy-sourced vitamins. Can you tell me about the importance of the actual sourcing, of where you get the vitamins, and everything that's in them?

MaryRuth: What's amazing is when you are making a product line, there's something called "private label", which somebody else has already made. People put their label on it. Then, there are custom blends. This is when you source a variety of different vitamins to make it a unique product.

My whole business is really a miracle story of when I wanted to create the custom blend, and source it, and make a liquid vitamin that was, for sure, sugar-free. Most of the liquid vitamins on the market have agave, or coconut sugar, or sucralose, or glucose, or different kinds of sugars. I said, "Okay, I want to make a sugar-free liquid vitamin. I want to source all the ingredients. I want to put a little bit of everything that someone would need."

It was unheard of, because at the time – this was about seven years ago – I was in a tremendous amount of debt. So, to launch a product in one of the most competitive industries, not just from zero funding, but from a deficit of that, is really hard because when you go to a manufacturer and you say, "I want to make this unique product," they will say, "Well, you need to pay half upfront for 25,000 bottles." We have many manufacturers all over the country now. But I convinced our first manufacturer, "Please, please, I have this practice. This is a really unique niche. I know that people will really appreciate this because it is sugar-free. If you give me a chance."

I had to call so many times to this one factory in California, speaking with this one woman, over and over again, who I'm still very close to now. I said, "I can only afford 100 bottles. So, can you please make a very small batch?" Even in the early first couple of years, we were making small batches every couple of days. Now, we do a couple major runs a month. It's different now. But what's amazing is that I convinced her. She sent, I think it was only 90 bottles to my apartment in New York City, which is across the street from my office. I would sell them only in my office to my clients.

Then I happened to put them on Amazon. And this was before Amazon was cool. I found out it was not cool when I was on an airplane with my husband, and someone said, "What do you do for a living?" I said, "I'm a nutritional consultant and certified health educator. I have a liquid supplement line that I sell on Amazon." My husband elbowed me and said, "No, don't say you're selling on Amazon. It sounds so cheap."

What's amazing is now, so many years later, I love it because it really equalized the playing field. So many people who want to do something, and they don't have a lot of funding, can launch a product on Amazon. It takes a lot of patience, a lot of energy. You have to be super organized. You have to follow the rules for sure or Amazon, like an algorithm, will eliminate your listing. We put it on Amazon in 2014. My clients gave me about 20 reviews. Then it went to the first page.

Jacqlyn: Wow!

MaryRuth: I sold gradually throughout that process. Again, it's because the other liquid supplements on the front of the page were not vegan, or not non-GMO, or gluten-free. The glycerin is what makes it taste sweet. It has been such an amazing process to read everyone's feedback. They definitely help people have more energy. Honestly, if they get their blood work done, they will see over time that they are doing really, really well.

Jacqlyn Burnett: Outside of vitamins, what can someone do who is just getting into mindful consuming?

MaryRuth: What do I recommend for someone who's just starting out, and they don't have a budget to buy vitamins? Chewing your food till it is liquid, not overeating, and not over-stuffing the stomach or the digestive tract. These are such powerful things. But it takes so much restriction and discipline to take the time to chew your food correctly.

Discipline and routine and structure is a form of self-love. It is a form of self-care. And sometimes, it takes a moment to think about, "You know what? I am going to exercise today. I'm going to stretch. I'm going to get ten minutes of sunshine, and then drink half my body weight in ounces in water. I'm going to really chew my food." Find the things that work best for you.

Jacqlyn Burnett: Thank you so much MaryRuth.

I start my day with mindfulness about my food choices. To kick off my morning, I drink a full glass of water, take my liquid vitamins, and head to the gym. When I return home, I mix up a delicious protein shake, and enjoy a hearty kale salad with homemade dressing. Fun fact: I've been enjoying salads for breakfast since 2017. Nourishing my body with essential vitamins and nutrients is a daily ritual that keeps me feeling my best. By starting the day with wholesome foods, I set myself up for success, and continue to make mindful choices throughout the day.

Just like your mindset can spiral, so can your gut. Your gut and brain are in constant communication and exist in symbiosis. To support your overall health, it is important to nourish your gut. Before I became plant-based in 2017, I used to eat egg whites with some type of green almost every morning. I switched to a plant-based diet when I realized that it was the best way for my body to operate. It was a quick decision that came after a significant realization. Here's how it happened.

I was put on ADD medication in fourth grade, and continued taking it until my last year of college. I tried different medications including Vyvance, Concerta, Ritalin, and Adderall, sometimes even taking two at once. After graduating college, I decided to cleanse my body of any substances that were not pure or organic. I was nervous about stopping the ADD medications, because I was unsure if my body was addicted to the stimulants I had taken for 13 years. ADD medications are also appetite suppressants, and since I had been taking them for so long, I didn't know if my normal eating pattern would return. As it turned out, my body was dependent on the medication. I struggled to get back on a normal bowel schedule, and tried everything from taking espresso shots to being prescribed MiraLAX for six months. Before going plant-based, I ate a healthy diet high in protein and vegetables. But it wasn't until I made the conscious decision to try something different, and go plant-based, that I finally got back on track. I share this story to show that every "body" is different; and it's important to figure out what works best for you. Do the research to understand how your choices may affect you. The bottom line is that a mindful, dense nutrient, wholesome lifestyle will support the optimization of your health.

    I share my knowledge, resources, and experiences with you so that you can benefit from my journey in health and wellness. I have been passionate about this field since the age of 14, and I continue to deepen my studies every day. It's not just for my own benefit, but for my family and loved ones as well.

By optimizing your diet, you can reduce stress and create more energy for growth. Switching to a more wholesome lifestyle, and being mindful of what you consume, will help you function smoothly in all areas of your life.

EXERCISE 6

The goal of this exercise is to help you practice mindful consuming.

First, take some time to reflect on your current eating habits. Are you generally mindful of what you eat? Or do you often find yourself mindlessly snacking on unhealthy foods? Do you tend to eat mostly processed and packaged foods? Or do you make a conscious effort to incorporate whole, unprocessed foods into your diet?

Next, over the course of a week, challenge yourself to become more mindful of what you eat. Pay attention to what you put in your body, and make a conscious effort to choose foods that are nutritionally beneficial, instead of filler foods that only provide temporary satisfaction.

As you go through this exercise, be patient with yourself. Remember that it may take some time to develop new habits. Your body creates enzymes to support your current system, so if you're making a major shift in your diet, you may notice some changes in the way you feel.

To help you stay on track, I recommend keeping a food diary where you record everything you eat and drink over the course of the week, along with any notable physical or emotional sensations you experience after each meal. This diary will also serve as a space for you to reflect on your overall experience with the exercise, and record any challenges you faced, or positive changes you noticed in your body, or your mood.

Remember, the goal of this exercise is not to deprive yourself of the foods you enjoy. Rather, to become more mindful of what you eat, and to make a conscious effort to choose foods that support your overall health and wellbeing. Feed yourself the good to feel the great. Keep in mind: You're a sports car, not a jalopy – feed your body the fuel it needs to run on premium!

Chapter 6
MINDSET MATTERS

"You are your only limit." —*Unknown*

Your mindset is everything. The way you think about life shapes your perspective; and ultimately, how you experience it. You have the power to choose whether you live in abundance or scarcity. Whether you see life happening to you, or through you. By operating from an abundant point of view, you open yourself up to more opportunities and joy for yourself and those around you. As we have explored in previous chapters, when we operate from a state of joy, all the shortages, voids, and blockages in our lives become mere illusions. So, let go of any limiting beliefs and embrace an abundant mindset – the possibilities are endless.

In 2014, my cousin, Josh, who lived in Los Angeles was having a birthday dinner. I was in Orange County, doing a summer internship. At 6:30 PM I grabbed his gift, a fitness outfit, got in my rental car, and started on my way. Just before I got to the

HAPPINESS HABITAT

freeway onramp, another vehicle ran a stop sign and slammed into my car at about 50 mph. The impact was so hard, it spun my car out of control. I hit two other cars before coming to a stop. The airbags exploded, and the birthday gift went flying. Out of the corner of my eye, I saw the guy who hit me regain his composure, then speed away. Thankfully, no one in the two cars I hit was seriously hurt. My car had sustained the most damage, and wasn't driveable. And I only suffered a bruised shoulder.

As all of us victims gathered, we remained calm. In this situation, I had the choice to react out of scarcity, or out of abundance. I decided I wasn't going to let the accident spoil my evening. I took all of the necessary steps to make sure the hit and run was handled, including getting my car towed and left in front of the rental lot to be dealt with tomorrow. I then continued on with my plans. As it fortuitously turned out, a friend of my roommate had seen the accident from across the road, and offered to drive me to my cousin's birthday dinner. She was heading that way anyway. The evening worked out. I made it to the birthday party (albeit an hour late) and was able to spend time with my cousin. This was all because I remained positive, handled the situation calmly, and operated from a state of abundance.

When we operate from abundance, we carry with us a sense of majesty and calmness. And a state of calmness allows us to experience life through a clear lens, with understanding. You can view the world as everything is happening to you, or through you. It is up to you to decide how you want to perceive the world. If you look at the world as life happening *through* you, the lessons that come from any experience will be much clearer, and more rewarding. When you make a point to find the lessons in every situation, you won't have to relearn them again. The lesson I learned in this situation was how to move through a bad accident with calmness and positivity. When you look for the light and lessons in every situation, you become a vessel for others, too.

HAPPINESS HABITAT

You don't just show up for yourself, but for all the people you get to be in front of. This is a beautiful responsibility we all get to have. Everyone has the ability to impact the room in a positive way and lift the mood, or negatively impact it. Be mindful of your conscious and unconscious state, and consider what it may be saying to others. The energy we emit when we enter a room can profoundly affect those around us. It is important to be aware of how we are impacting the environment. By operating from a state of love and abundance, we can spread positivity and uplift those in our presence. Embrace the power you have to make a positive impact on those around you.

That accident I was involved in, if I had operated from a state of fear, panic, and scarcity, imagine how that would have impacted the situation. Had I not remained calm, those around me would have become chaotic as well. Because I came from a place of abundance, and knew everything was going to be okay, I was able to be there for others, too.

HAPPINESS HABITAT

Remember: Your circumstances do not define you. It is your perception and response to the world that shapes your experiences. Appreciate the present moment, and use it as an opportunity to learn, and grow. Embrace your power to define your circumstances, and make a positive impact on those around you.

Your lens is crucial in shaping how you experience the world. By viewing the world through a lens of love and positivity, you enrich your own life and inspire others. When you operate from a place of love, you will attract love. When you operate from a place of kindness, you will attract kindness. Your mindset shapes your experiences in the world. You only have this moment. Make it the best it can be. Gratitude gives you perspective. Be grateful for the present, and know that you have the power to change it as you wish.

Having a positive and abundant mindset is crucial to maximizing your potential. When you operate from a place of positivity, you attract positivity, and remain open to new opportunities. When you are open, it is easier to see the potential in every experience, rather than being negative and closed off. Think of it like this: When your palms are closed, you cannot receive anything. But when they're open, you can receive anything. As I said before, my friend, Garrain Jones, shared this metaphor with me while I was with him at his home in his inspiration room. Each room in his home has a unique purpose and intention. He went from living out of his car, to becoming a high-level transformational coach working with thousands of people.

Positivity and openness allow us to receive the gifts of life. You cannot receive these gifts when you are closed off. Cultivating an abundance mindset doesn't happen overnight. It starts with the *decision* to live a joyful and abundant life. It is the "consistent and persistent pursuit of your potential," David Meltzer, likes to say. I will share some practices that can help shift your mindset to one of abundance through your actions, words, and thoughts. Our thoughts influence our words, and our words influence our actions.

You are empowered and abundant. You are who you say you are. Be confident in your beliefs and values, and everything else will fall into place.

Read the following affirmations out loud:

"I am joy."

"I am love."

"I am abundance."

The words we use are powerful. They influence our 40,000 daily thoughts, and shape our mindset, perspective, and reality. Every single word we hear and say carries energy, and within that energy carries data. That data is sent to our subconscious and fed to our conscious. All of our words carry a vibration. A simple way to raise our vibration, and influence our subconscious, and our surroundings, is by always speaking positive, uplifting words. You are who you say you are. Be purposeful with your words, and your words will materialize your intentions. The energy that is transmitted in what you say will emanate through the rest of your being. We can use our words to influence our surroundings through affirmations, gratitude, and the messages we convey.

For example, instead of saying "I'm sorry" when you make a mistake, say "Thank you for understanding" to reinforce a state of abundance, rather than lack. When you say, "I'm sorry" you are coming from the energy or state of "not enough". Now, I'm not saying that you do not take responsibility for your actions. Rather, *how* you take responsibility, and the frequency that it emits is so important. What if you replaced every "I'm sorry" with "Thank you for understanding"? Try it now. Do you feel the difference?

Imagine you are in the car on your way to meet a friend for lunch. Suddenly, heavy traffic slows you down, and you arrive 20 minutes late. You might feel frustrated and agitated, but instead of apologizing and rehashing the negative experience, you could choose to speak from a place of gratitude. Instead of saying "I'm sorry" and bringing down your vibration with negativity, you could say something like, "Thank you so much for waiting for me. I've been looking forward to our lunch!" This simple change in perspective can improve your present moment, and create a positive ripple effect that continues to improve your experience of life. By choosing to speak from a place of abundance and gratitude, you can influence your mindset and raise your vibration.

One simple way to change your mindset is to change the words you use. For example, instead of saying "I have to" do something, try saying "I get to" do it instead. Rather than "I have to take the trash out," say "I get to take the trash out." This subtle change will shift your perspective from one of scarcity to one of abundance.

HAPPINESS HABITAT

This is a shift that happens when we consciously observe ourselves. Whenever you catch yourself thinking a negative thought, try using the technique of "Cancel, Clear, and Connect". My dad taught me this a long time ago, and it has stuck with me since. Say "Cancel" to stop yourself from carrying the thought. Then "Clear" to break the connection with it. And "Connect" to reconnect with your center and move forward from a higher frequency. The "Cancel – Clear – Connect" technique will cultivate an abundance mindset, and enhance your experiences.

One of my greatest mentors is my cousin, **David Meltzer**. I'm lucky to have instilled his beliefs on mindset and perspective. David is the co-founder of Sports 1 Marketing and formerly served as CEO of the renowned Leigh Steinberg Sports & Entertainment agency, which was the inspiration for the movie *Jerry Maguire*. He is a three-time international best-selling author, a Top 100 Business Coach, the executive producer of Entrepreneur's #1 digital business show, *The Two Minute Drill,* and host of the top entrepreneur podcast, *The Playbook.* David has been recognized by *Variety Magazine* as their Sports Humanitarian of the Year, and was awarded the Ellis Island Medal of Honor.

I interviewed him on my podcast back when I was living with him during the early months of Covid. I'll share with you our conversation. I'm sure it will have a profound impact on you, the same way it has for me. It holds many lessons, and is a dynamic story of what can happen when you take stock in who you are, and shift your mindset to allow yourself to live your truth.

> **Jacqlyn:** Welcome to the Happiness Habitat podcast. Today I am joined by a very special guest. Someone who I've not only looked up to for years, but he's also my cousin, David Meltzer.
>
> **David:** I've been looking forward to this, watching your evolution and revolution all in one. So thanks for having me on your show.

Jacqlyn: Yes. That's what you have created so beautifully for yourself and your family. It's been amazing. I want to start out by talking about your transformation. I know you went from becoming super successful and wealthy at a very young age, to losing it all, then building it back again. I know it really well, but for people listening, it's just a tremendous story, and I'm so excited to have you share it.

David: Well, it's really about my relationship to money. Since I grew up with nothing, but super happy, I thought that money bought happiness and love. My journey was reaffirmed all through my childhood, my college years, my law school years, and into my professional years, until my first warning at age 30. Everything in my life was indicative that money would buy love and happiness. I wanted to buy my mom a house, because that was the only time I'd see her not happy. She was financially stressed because she had six kids. And, being a single mom, that was a lot of pressure. So, in my mind, I was focused subconsciously, unconsciously, and consciously on making money. And like I said, it was reaffirmed every step of my career. From girls I dated, to the girl I got engaged to when I was law school. To being able to marry my dream girl, and break it off with my fiancée in thinking that she loved me because I finally made it.

After all those different things, and nine months of law school, I was a millionaire. I bought my mom a house and a car. I went to Silicon Valley, made more millions in the middleware space. Then became a CEO of the world's first smartphone. Everybody sucked up to me. Everyone told me how great I was. I thought that everyone loved me. I thought that I was so happy. Then at 30 years old, my dad gave me the first type of warning.

HAPPINESS HABITAT

My dad, who left when I was five, broke my heart when I was 10. He lied to me, telling me that he didn't forget my birthday, when in fact he did. He said he didn't believe in birthdays. So, I had this hatred for him because he was a liar, a cheater, manipulator, back-end seller, and at 30, he gave me my first present in 20 years. That present ended up saving my life, but not that day. I ended up hating my father even more because he gave me a jacket, and I thought he was punishing me.

He gave me a sports coat that had no pockets in it. And I remember specifically being so excited at first, thinking my dad had changed. That my dad had learned some great lesson. But no, he was trying to teach me a lesson, and I was the one who was lost. At 30, he told me he gave me a jacket to hang in my closet, to remind me that money doesn't buy love or happiness. He told me that I couldn't take anything with me when I was gone, and I was just like him, so he was concerned for me. At that time, I was in ego-based consciousness with the need to be right. The need to be offended, separate, superior, angry, frustrated. So, I told him to f' off. I told him that I was nothing like him. That he was a liar, a cheater, a manipulator. I hung the jacket in my closet, and forgot about it.

Six years later, I went golfing. I was now running the most notable sports agency in the world. It was the inspiration for the Tom Cruise movie, *Jerry McGuire*... you know, "Show me the money!" Once again, reaffirming money buys love and happiness. I literally got hired because I was an icon to make money in financial security of teaching young athletes that their son or daughter would be taken care of financially, because I was an expert at that. I was Midas.

HAPPINESS HABITAT

I went golfing with "John", my best friend since the fourth grade. It was when I met my future wife, Julie, as well. In fact, in sixth grade, John asked Julie for me if she wanted to go study together. She said, "No. Tell him to ask me himself." Once again, though, she ended up marrying me after years and years of not liking me, or even hating me.

Anyway, John and I went golfing, and I asked him, "Why don't you ever want to hang out with me? Hey, why don't you come to the Super Bowl, or The Masters with me? Hangout with these celebrities and athletes." John was a pretty straightforward guy, and he says, "I don't like who you hang out with. And I don't like what you guys are doing." It really hurt my feelings. I said, "I don't do what those guys do." John just looked at me and said, "Dave, you can lie to me, just don't lie to yourself."

HAPPINESS HABITAT

That really hurt. He was the first person in a long time that, since my dad six years earlier, had told me the truth. Somebody who wasn't just telling me what I wanted to hear, being a "yes" person in my life. Even my wife was probably too afraid to tell me the truth, because she had so much to lose. Because I was a great provider, and I was basically a good person, but I was just lost.

Two weeks later, though, my wife had had it. I went and lied to her for the last time. I went to the Grammy Awards with a rapper named Lil Jon, and changed clothes in the car, and came home at 5:30 in the morning, drunk, high, and completely lost. My wife told me she wasn't happy, and she was going leave me, and I better take stock in who I was and what I wanted to become, or I probably was going to end up dead.

I got really angry. Same reaction I had with my dad six years earlier. It was all about them. How dare they? How dare they question the great...? What have I ever done, but provide for all of them? I was so successful, I was so happy, I was so great, and I went to bed angry.

The next morning, I woke up even more upset. I was going to take everything. I was living in a mindset of "My world for me." I ventured off to the world of "not enough", of being a victim. But no, everything was "for me." I was buying things that I didn't need. I was trying to impress people I didn't like. And I forgot about what was really important. So, I was going to find out who the best lawyer was that could help me take everything, including my kids.

Jacqlyn: Oh my gosh.

David: I was so mad, so offended, so resentful. I felt like, *How dare she!* And I looked over, and in the closet, a jacket just called out to me. I looked at it and ... I still get choked up ... I was thinking, *I'm just like my dad.* The last person I wanted to be.

Jacqlyn: That makes me wanna cry.

David: Yes. I was a liar, cheater, manipulator, back-end seller. So I wrote down those values, and took stock of who I was. I've been taking inventory of my values every day since. Not afraid to see I was being a hypocrite, and then to change, to accelerate, to grow. But 13 years later, I've been able to manifest everything I want in my life by being of service and value, by living to pursue the truth.

I know that I'm not 100% to my potential. And I don't think anyone is. I'm okay illuminating my mistakes, and teaching other people to find the light, love, and lessons. And everything that they're doing, in the same way, I still find the light, love and lessons, and everything like that.

Jacqlyn: Amazing. Every time I hear this story, I choke up.

David: Me too. And I have to tell it all the time.

Jacqlyn: It's just like what you say, truth vibrates the fastest, and you literally strike a chord when you're just sharing your truth, and that is your truth. I want to touch on what that moment was like when you lost everything? What was it like when you really were having to build these conscientious values that you have now? Because, like a lot of people, they're still growing, they're still learning how to build and live to their truth.

David: Yes, it's interesting, because when I learned to look within, I now had things that I couldn't control. When I was looking for acceptance and love and appreciation and worthiness from others, I wouldn't ever get it. Because you can only give what you have. So, I started looking within. And two years after I went through my transformation, and made a quantum shift, as I call it, is when I lost everything.

I lost everything, but I was prepared. In fact, I think that's what scared my wife the most is how calm I was. I was finally living in control. I controlled my mindset, my feelings, what I thought and said and did. I controlled all those things. And I was super confident that I'd be able to take care of everything. I was now living by my own values. And I was not trying to please anyone else but myself, so I could give it to someone else.

I'm always that way now. In fact, the lessons keep coming. Two and a half years ago, I asked my wife, "What would you like? I'll give you anything, I appreciate you so much for everything that we have. What do you want?" And she said, "For you to take care of yourself." Because I wasn't, physically, or health-wise. She said, "If you take care of yourself, I know you'll take care of everyone else."

That's where I was in 2008, I had to take care of myself. That's why receiving is so important. Feeling worthy. I teach people all the time, I see them using guilt in offense, and resentment in their "wise" excuses, in their ego, their pride, their separateness. They're in fear, all the time as an excuse. Because they're not tough enough just to deal with themselves. They're not tough enough to receive, and they can make every excuse: "Oh, I just give everything to everyone else." What are you giving to everyone else? If you don't have anything, what are you really giving? C'mon, get tough. Go get something, and then give it away. To me, that's unconditional giving. You could sit at home, getting high on your couch, and tell yourself that you do everything for everyone else. But what are you really doing?

I got cousins and family and friends who are just like that. They're like these philanthropic humanitarians: "Oh, I care about the environment." I'm like, okay, so what are you doing besides flapping your lips, and telling people to recycle? Preaching and literally putting judgments on things. You want to change the environment? Then create something that converts plastic into energy. Or donate a boatload of money, like Jeff Bezos: $10 billion to save our environment. That seems to me like a good way to do it. And those are the types of perspectives that I teach. Those are the ones that I live by: To give and receive are one. Receiving by itself is no good, and giving by itself is no good.

Jacqlyn: What are some good practices that someone can apply to fill themselves?

David: I have five practices that I believe in, and apply in my own life. As I said, giving and receiving is one. I love the way that you use the word "practice", because it is a focused practice, especially for people who are younger. Patience is a virtue. And respect that everything is a practice. And we want, especially now, instant gratification. We want to be able to see and materialize immediate acceleration and change and growth. But that's just not possible. Our senses aren't that strong. Our memories are even weaker. The growth doesn't occur that way. It occurs slowly and exponentially. And you have to be willing to put the work in.

So, the five things to practice. Number one: Take inventory of your values –

personal, experiential, giving and receiving.

Two: You need to learn the "ask and attract" methodology. You need to learn to ask a series of questions of how you can be of service or value. But also a series of questions knowing that there are no gatekeepers. That there are only power sponsors, and sponsored people. A sponsor is someone that knows someone who can do something for you, or someone who can help you. Or a power sponsor is someone who can actually help you themselves, with something or someone, or they know something or someone.

Third one's a big one for me, which is the hardest practice and the most quantitatively valuable in one's life, because it blends time: And that's being a student of your calendar. People misinterpret this, I probably have said this a thousand times. But studying is not just looking on your calendar. Most people look at their calendar every day, but let alone study it, which is pay attention to and give intention to the coincidences that you want. If you do that, if you study what you have planned in the day, with a what I call the Meltzer Kaleidoscope, a lens of creativity, accessibility, and gratitude. If you study that productivity, or you study the accessibility: How are you accessing things? How are you accessible to others? And then there's gratitude, which gives you a gracious lens, gives you the ability to take pain for what it is.

Jacqlyn: Please explain.

David: Sure. What pain is, all it is, is an indicator. It's like the hazard lights, or your engine light comes on. It's an indicator of pain that says, "Hey, buddy, you got a lesson to learn – physical, emotional, spiritual, or a financial lesson to learn." Yet, we can't see it that way. We see it as a stop, resistance, a shortage, an obstacle in the way. But it's not. It's just an indicator that there's something you need to learn.

The lens of gratitude is so important, because it allows you to see the primary pain as fear. And all the secondary emotions that go behind it. Those needs of the ego that I spill off all the time about: The need to be right, the need to be superior, separate, anxious, angry – all those things.

The fourth practice is simple: "Do it now." That's a mathematical advantage in the universe. It's easy, 100% of the things you do now get done. People get stuff done, and ahead of people who don't. You can even have a secondary list of things you can't get done right away, and put those in as a student of your calendar for the next day. And prioritize by what's most important first, it's urgent, just delegating somebody.

Then finally, the fifth and most important in life, especially if you're young, is to practice empathy. So, practicing empathy is a three-step process. One, when an indicator of pain comes up, is to stop. That's the most ferocious free will that you'll ever have. If anybody's ever been in the ego-based consciousness, "in the throes of the wrong trajectory," as I call it, and you're able to stop, it's amazing. Then, after you're so ferocious, you need to be a Buddha. So I call myself "the ferocious Buddha". Buddha is centered and neutral. So, stop, drop, and drop out, or go neutral. Breath in through your nose, out through your mouth.

And then finally, roll. That is, take action. Move into the right direction, in alignment with the values that you have. So, you roll toward the objectives that you've set forth by taking inventory of your values every day. If you are able to raise your consciousness, you're on fire, mind, body, and soul: On fire. If you're on fire, you establish an amount of confidence: Stop, drop and roll.

Those are the five things that you can do to have that life-changing practice. And I promise you, it will work.

Jacqlyn: You've instilled these practices in me, all the way back at Sport 1 Marketing, when I worked for you. Even the D-I-N, the Do It Now practice, if it takes under five minutes, do it now. Be a student of your calendar. Know everything you're doing that's paid, unpaid, and just be grateful for the journey. For people who are on their journey that are so attached to, "I need to make a million dollars by 25!" Or, "I need to do XYZ."

How do you detach from that, because that can really halt you.

David: It's even harder when you love someone a ton. I've had relatives like you who worked for me at 20 years old. My own nephew, as well. And it takes a lot of patience to allow someone to learn... To know as long as it takes to get something done. Meaning there's no "overnight successes". I can't make you learn. All I can do is expose you to different ways of thinking.

Denis Waitley helped me a lot. He's an older, famous sales motivator and educator. He's written books that are incredible. He talks about taking the position of planting seeds for trees we will never sit under. Even when you were 20 years old, graduated college, and were a go-getter ... the best definition I have for them is, "People that don't know what they don't know." And at 20 years old, everybody's so worried what everybody else thinks. Then at 40 years old, what you'll find is: "You don't care what anybody thinks." And at 60 years old, what I find is that, I'm not 60 yet, but what people realize is: "Nobody cares." That's the progression of life.

So, at 20 years old, how do you teach somebody who doesn't know what they don't know? What you can do is plant seeds, water the seeds that have been planted, or help the tree grow, and harvest as much as you can. It's so much fun, because I don't quit on people, just like I don't quit on my potential. So, it's a joy to watch your evolution, and your boyfriend Casey Adams' evolution, and my nephew, Josh's evolution. And you guys are still just in your mid-twenties. And I'm someone who plays a major role in my company. I'm 52. I have almost been working twice as long as you guys have been alive.

Jacqlyn: That's a while!

David: Right? And that's a lot of experience. I'm a very focused person. It's not like there's activity, I get paid for an activity. I don't, and you have to have that perspective of what you're doing, and who you're doing it with, and allow things to happen.

Jacqlyn: I am still reaping the benefits from what I've learned from you five years ago. I'm so grateful. And I'm still reaping the benefits from my environment that my parents created for me when I was very young. They instilled in me so many beautiful values, my dad for example would always say to my brother and I, "You're an asset to this planet!" And he'd repeat that over and over again to us, still today. Now, it's not like it's made my head big, but it encouraged me to think, "How can I be an asset to this planet?" How can I give back?" I want to talk about the environment that you've created for yourself. I don't know, I want to call it happiness habitat, but I'm sure happy here! How have you created such a beautiful environment? People say the grass is always greener on the other side, or it's greener where you water it. So how do you make the grass greener?

David: Don't forget, the grass may be greener on the other side, but you still got to cut it.

Jacqlyn: Ha!

David: That's the work. You have to enjoy the consistent, persistent, pursuit of your potential. I gave a talk today about how we give meaning to everything that we see. If you read Victor Frankel's book – he was a Holocaust survivor – Frankel talks about giving meaning to everything that he sees.

I believe if you're stuck, you're lucky. Because that means you're trying to grow, and it means you're trying to grow more than the speed in which you're growing. That's all stuck is. And people who don't feel stuck aren't trying to grow. You could be locked in a room, and if you never tried to get out, you wouldn't feel stuck. If you're nice and cozy, if there's the TV, the X-box, Instagram, and YouTube videos ... if I built a closet like this, and it has everything I need for comfort in there, I don't feel stuck. But the minute I tried to get out of there and it doesn't open, now I feel stuck. What if every time I tried to pull the door open, it just moved a micro millimeter. And then the second time, it was twice as much as that, and then third time, it was twice as much more. What if, at the fifth time, I'm saying, "I'm stuck! I'm going to quit!" And I just go back to living in my closet. That sucks, but that's what many people do with their lives.

The external situations that change, sometimes faster and sometimes slower, in which we anticipate, are irrelevant. They are irrelevant because we give meaning to everything we see. As long as you're consistently, persistently pursuing your potential and enjoying that, it's just stuck being stuck. I'm always stuck being stuck, because I'm constantly trying to accelerate and grow. And I rejoice in it. I love it.

I even have shifted my paradigm of pain into the fact that I get excited, and a new joy comes on. Because it means there's a big lesson for me. I just pray that learning the lessons of the physical and financial pain, those are two that I try not to experience too often – I don't feel as if financially I need to grow and experience big pains anymore. So, I'm a little bit more cautious, and physically as well. I don't jump motorcycles off the roofs to learn lessons, like 19-year-old David Jäger. I don't want to do dangerous things like that anymore. But spiritually, emotionally, I want just enough pain physically to keep in shape and grow. Because I think a certain kind of pain can be exciting, and good, too.

Jacqlyn: Sometimes, my lens of gratitude, when I have painful moments ... like I had a little painful moment this morning, and I recognized it, and I thought, okay, this means I'm transforming right now. That's how I recognized it. But sometimes we don't always want to have those stuck feelings, or sometimes we don't get to experience those feelings. What's a way to go into that growth zone, even if it's not through perceived paid?

David: I think two things always work ... First, understanding. You've got to be patient to understand. I seek the truth. I pursue the truth. If I'm in one of those situations, I just try to understand it, give it time, but I'm aggressive. I'm ferocious in understanding, and I make a point to be "more interested than interesting." That means being a good listener, instead of trying to talk all the time.

Then two, I pray for its happiness. I give it the light, the love, the lessons, the energy that it deserves. I know that I'm being completely vulnerable, like you said earlier, and then I'm invulnerable.

Telling the truth, and when I don't tell the truth, I have good intentions when I don't tell the whole truth. There are shortages and obstacles, and interference or collision, to the greatest source of power, the lessons that I have. And the more that I keep learning it, the greater my awareness. The greater my awareness, the easier life gets. It's very simple.

Jacqlyn: That's beautiful. Thank you, Dave. I have one last question for you. How do you define happiness?

David: That's easy: "To enjoy the consistent every day, persistent without quitting, pursuit of your potential." Happiness is the greatest disease, the strongest disease shared by everyone simply by witnessing it, and it will strengthen everyone's immune system. My mission in life, as you know, is to empower over a billion people to be happy. So, I'm so glad that you're one of my 1,000 people. And I know I'm empowering another 1,000 to empower another 1,000 to be happy, and 1,000 times 1,000 is a million. A million times 1,000 is a billion. And together we create a collective consciousness of happiness so that the world is a Happiness Habitat.

Jacqlyn: Beautiful. Thank you, Dave.

Your mindset changes when you change. When you are aware of how you can grow, and are grateful for the present. You already have what you need to grow. Now it's time to grow with what you have. Your mindset is the fundamental tool for everything else you create. Your mindset is like the soil. You can either grow weeds, or you can grow oak trees.

EXERCISE 7

For the next week, pay attention to your thoughts, words, and reactions. Ask yourself whether you are coming from a place of love, or fear. Whenever you can, replace the words "have" or "need" with "get" to shift your perspective toward abundance. At the end of each day, write down any lessons you have learned, and reflect on them. Notice any changes in your perspective, or mindset. Then take time to realign with your goals and intentions. This exercise will help you cultivate a more positive and empowering outlook on life.

Chapter 7
COMMUNICATION TO CONNECTION

"Communication - the human connection - is the key to personal and career success." — Paul J. Meyer

The human race is a social species, and humans have the extraordinary ability to forge meaningful connections through communication. It's this capacity for connection that drives us toward achieving success in our careers, and relationships – turning dreams into realities. Becoming fluent in expressing our thoughts and feelings clearly, within ourselves as well as with others, will unlock a world of opportunities, where boundaries are broken down by understanding one another better. Communication: It's an incredibly powerful tool when used proficiently!

Words have a special power. They form the basis of our relationships, and shape how we are perceived by others. Sometimes it's not always what you say, but what the other person *hears*. The more certain you are in your values, beliefs, and desires, the more your words will come through clearly. There are many roles we play in communicating. When it comes to communication, the most important criteria is clarity. Effective and clear communication is the exchange of thoughts, ideas, and heartfelt knowledge. It's optimized by leveraging our whole consciousness; our body language, our tone, and our spoken word.

    I am grateful to have grown up with people who helped form my communication style. My father was a successful business owner, and his career was based upon communication strategies. My father's effective and clear style of communication spilled over to me. If there was a more efficient, clear way to convey a message, he would help me to see that. He taught me that communication in its barest essence was attractive. He learned from his dad, also a great communicator, who instilled in him the overruling law that "It's not what you say –

it's *how* you say it." When you distill that down, it ends up being an extremely powerful lesson.

The posture you convey expresses a lot of the message. Your tone carries emotion, and that emotion generates a chemical reaction in your body that helps us understand the message. In other words, how you carry the message is louder than the words themselves. Whenever you talk, you have the opportunity to speak with certainty or confusion, joy or frustration. It's very easy to tell one from the other, and the energy that is conveyed when doing either. My dad taught me that communication is based on my own self-awareness, values, and true beliefs. This was the basis of my education in communication. I always try to make sure that my inner world matches how I show up on the outside. I stand tall, enunciate clearly, and always speak with a smile on my face.

Body language is a powerful form of communication that predates spoken language. Many politicians and other public figures hire body language coaches to help them convey a more sincere, caring, and honest image to their audiences. According to research by Albert Mehrabian, a pioneer in the study of body language, the total impact of a message is about 7% verbal (words only), and 38% vocal (including tone of voice, inflection, and other sounds), with the remaining 55% coming from nonverbal cues like body language (*NY Times*). Your body language reflects your inner emotional state. By paying attention to it, you can better understand others, and communicate more effectively.

For example, a person who is afraid might fold their arms, look down, or cross their legs. While someone who is confident will stand up straight with their shoulders back, smile, and keep their arms at their sides. When you understand a person's emotional state, listen to what they are saying, and note their situational context, you can distinguish between fiction and fact, and interact with others in a way that is authentic and meaningful.

HAPPINESS HABITAT

When you communicate from a place of love, you will receive love if those you are communicating with also love themselves. On the other hand, when you communicate from a state of fear, you will attract fear, simply because that is the message you are sending out. Just as we learned in the Quantum Physics chapter, like vibrations attract each other. The frequency you operate on will return to you like a boomerang. The world has a beautiful way of showing you who you really are, and giving you exactly what you desire and intend, along with all the light, love, and lessons that come with it. Knowing your values, and being certain of yourself, will lead to the same interaction in return. Communication is how you convey messages, both spoken and unspoken. All of your emotions will show up through the way you communicate.

Before you begin to communicate, know your worth, remind yourself of who you are, and operate from a state of kindness. When you operate from a state of kindness and love, your messages and body language are much stronger and more powerful than when you show up from a place of fear or uncertainty.

Which type of stranger would you rather interact with: Someone who is looking down, sluggish, and speaks very softly? Or someone who is standing tall, speaking with confidence, and smiling? The second person is operating on a higher frequency, and this level of frequency will be returned. This is how I have learned to operate. I often check in with my values and beliefs, and come from a place of love. It's all a practice. Even as I type these words, I am sitting up a little taller, and my mind is becoming more attuned to how I can better serve you, the reader.

With your body language, tone of voice, and words, you can "trick" your mind into thinking you are feeling a certain way, and release certain "happy" chemicals in your brain. For example, if you are feeling out of sorts, not on center, you can try smiling and standing up straight to manipulate your mind into thinking you are happy. This will release serotonin and make you feel better. Operating at a higher level means being aligned with who you are, and communicating in a way that reflects your emotions. This can help you attract like-minded people, and improve the effectiveness of your communication. Remember, you are like a boomerang. You will attract like frequency!

    Effective communication is crucial not only in your interactions with others, but also with yourself. Speaking up and expressing your thoughts and feelings is essential. My significant other, **Casey Adams**, has built a successful career in the field of communication. He has interviewed some of the most influential thought-leaders in the world, including Larry King, Maye Musk, Robert Greene, and Marc Randolph, among others. He's one of the most in-tune humans I know. He has been able to meet with the greatest minds in our society by effectively communicating with himself and others. I formally sat down with Casey to dive into what has made him such a profound communicator.

> **Jacqlyn**: Can you tell me, at the fundamental level, why is communication with yourself so important?

> **Casey**: Communicating with yourself is such a powerful state to live in, because at the end of the day, we are continuously speaking to ourselves. Telling ourselves things that are positive or negative, and just analyzing our lives every single day. Your self-talk and that internal communication dictates every outcome of your life. Whether that's telling yourself you do or don't want to go to the gym. Telling yourself that you will or won't run a marathon. To starting that business and communicating to yourself your own self- confidence.

For me, since I was 16 years old, coming from small town in Virginia, and having had a neck brace injury, I dealt with negative self-talk for the longest time. There was a period where I didn't think I was good enough, and I didn't know what I wanted to do. I had no confidence. And, as time went on, I learned the importance of not only positive self-talk, but self-talk overall. Through all the different interviews I've done, through the different conversations, it all comes back to oneself, and how you take information and transform that into how you think, and what you tell yourself.

Jacqlyn: How can you go from negative self-talk to really getting in the habit of speaking to yourself in such a positive, kind light? As someone who is so close to me, I really get to observe you every single day. You are genuinely the most positive, kind person I know. And even in negative situations that we experience sometimes together, whether you experience it as negative or not, you always have a positive outlook. And you always speak to yourself so highly. So, how do you go from being in that so-called negative environment to speaking well of yourself, and staying in that positivity?

Casey: When it comes to positive or negative self-talk, I don't look at myself as someone that's always positive. But I always have a positive perspective. And I think there's a huge difference there of when you see someone you love do something great, you can think, "That's a positive situation." For me, I think it's just framing it around the perspective, because your perspective can change so much.

Over the years, I've learned how to always have a positive perspective on things. That doesn't mean that I'm always positive, by any means. But the perspective of positivity comes through gratitude. Being grateful for all of the little things. For example, I have two legs and I can run. I am healthy. I feel great. I have beautiful relationships in my life, including you. And if you take all of the things that are important to you, and you can say, "Wow, my life is great!" it frames your perspective on positivity so much easier. Because, you could be going through things in business that are not good, that are not positive. But, if you can bring that positive perspective into every aspect of life, it allows you to think clearly. Also, to make more calculated decisions. And it helps you to stay on track with whatever it is that you're doing.

If I was to give practical feedback, or advice on how to live a life with a positive perspective, outside of the gratitude points I just brought up, it would be to take time to really think about, and write down, what's important to you in life. Like a couple of key things that I mentioned were family, health, and relationships. It allows me then, when I'm going through something that might be challenging, to instantaneously go check on those three things. If those things are great or good, then everything else in my life feels less – not less important. But I don't have to stress about it, knowing that my top priorities are okay. And everything else is more so as a mental challenge to get better, and to persevere through whatever it may be.

Jacqlyn: When you encounter situations that aren't so positive, how do you manage and go through those situations?

Casey: I go through many times, very often – I mean, you know this more than anyone –when things are hard, whether that's business or physical. And I go through phases like everyone where I get down on myself. I have that negative self-talk. What allows me to get back to my baseline of a positive perspective is simply identifying that I'm having this negative self-talk. I've learned to be able to detect that very quickly. Also, it's a blessing to experience that, right?

For example, running a marathon. I ran my first marathon in December 2022. Going into that experience, I knew that not only was it going to be so mentally taxing and physically challenging, but the self-talk that I was about to go through wasn't going to always be positive the whole time. I knew that going into it. And I think that's also something powerful, where with a business venture, with a relationship like you and I have, you have to go into situations knowing that it's not always going to be perfect. That you are going to — I don't think the right word is — suffer. But in any situation in life, you will deal with suffering. And sometimes it is extreme. Sometimes it is not so extreme. Very subtle.

And back to the marathon example, like knowing that things are going to suck. On mile one, you're going to be feeling great, the energy is there, and you're all positive, you're excited. Versus mile 21 for me was a mile of suffering, of negative self-talk, of "Oh my gosh, can I do this? Can I maintain this pace? Can I keep pushing? I have never gone this distance before in this territory of the unknown." And I think you learn the most about yourself in situations of the unknown, from new experiences, because if you are just repeating the same actions and experiences, typically you're going to feel the same emotions, right?

If you're someone who knows that "Oh, I eat sugar, then I feel positive," you're probably going to know this going into that situation. Versus, if you know that "Oh, when I go work out, I get down on myself because I'm overweight, and I feel bad about myself," you probably are going to retract from that. But that's the moment and the times where you can learn the most about yourself. And going back to my first point, start to learn how to call out and identify when you're having that negative self-talk.

To summarize, learn to identify negative self-talk quickly. You can get your experience of doing that by putting yourself in situations that are new, that are difficult, that are just different from what you're typically used to on a daily basis.

Jacqlyn: You've used communication as a means of a tool in business as well, such as your podcast, *The Casey Adams Show*, interviewing influential leaders like Larry King, Robert Greene, Maye Musk and I think over 400 notable people. You've used the tool of communication to get you to the point of being in front of a microphone with those powerful people. How have you used communication to actually get to that point, to get in front of the microphone with these guests? Because getting someone such as a Larry King on the podcast, or Maye Musk on your show, isn't such an easy thing to do. How have you used the tool of communication to get you there?

Casey: Since the beginning of my career, communication has been such a powerful aspect of, not just my career, but really *everyone's* career. I've never met anyone that's gotten anything out of life who hasn't been, to some degree, an effective communicator. It starts with self-communication, like we've talked about. Setting a goal. Being determined. And knowing initially that you are capable, and believing in that. That's confident communication.

When I started the podcast, my number one goal was not only, "How do I communicate with these people?" But, "How can I use this medium of communication to learn something new? To meet interesting people? And build a brand that I can communicate to the world?" When it comes to your brand, all you're doing with building a brand is communicating a certain message and feeling to the world. And I wanted to communicate that not only am I having great conversations, but it's impactful listening in a sense.

Over the years of interviewing 400 people, the number one reason I was able to get in front of these guests was, yes, by communicating. But more so, by having clear, effective communication. For example, when you have a podcast and want to sit down with someone, you might presume they're getting so many messages. Some of my past guests like Rick Ross or Larry King, you might already guess, they're very busy. And in order to get their attention, you have to effectively communicate. What does that mean? That means being very straight to the point and value driven.

An example I like to share is the story of when I reached out to Rick Ross. The way I communicated to him to get him to come on my podcast was simple and effective. I said, "Hey, Rick Ross, I would love to have you on my podcast for 15 minutes to promote your new book. I also recently had on your favorite author, Robert Greene. He said to tell you hello," or something along those lines. But overall, that was the meat of the message. I always reflect on that because when I interviewed him, I asked Rick Ross, "Why did you come on my podcast?" And he told me, "You presented yourself like a boss." There's a clip out there on the Internet where he shares why, and says something like, "It was coming with value, not coming with my hands out." I shared the value of promoting his book, gave the amount of time it would take, and shared a mutual warm lead. That level of communication was simple and effective, and it got his attention. Hearing that from him only reassured my perspective of what effective communication is.

And that's just one example. If I were to summarize how I got in front of all of these people? It's coming with clear objectives, and being value driven. Because with any conversation, whether that's with oneself, with your significant other, or with someone you want to have on your podcast, you want to have clear communication. Be very transparent. And come with value. Whether that's value in the sense of doing something exciting, doing something great for them, or having a platform to promote someone's book on your podcast, for example.

Equally important, which I won't dive too deep in right now, is being consistent. Sometimes you could be the best communicator, but if someone doesn't hear it, or have the opportunity to hear your message, it's like they never heard it. And being consistent, especially from the standpoint of social media, and reaching out to people from a business perspective. It's very important. If anything, it's more important, to be consistent, so that your message can actually be heard.

Jacqlyn: Wow, thank you so much. If you had to share your three best tools to being a better and more effective communicator, what would those be?

Casey: Number one: Be extremely clear with your message. Being clear means getting to the point and having a goal to what you are saying.

Number two: Be authentic. This is by far the most important aspect of communication. You can read a million books and try to master the art of communication, but at the end of the day, you are you, and you have to be authentic with who you are. You can take different ideas and lessons from people, but always remain yourself. And by "remain yourself", I mean what works for me isn't going to be exactly what works for you. And what works for you is going to make you, you. So, embrace yourself, be authentic. Whether you're speaking to yourself, speaking to a crowd, or reaching out to someone over a cold email, be you and be authentic.

Number three: Think of communication as an art, because it is your entire life. You will be communicating in all different contexts, from relationships, to business, to your romantic partner. And we've talked about some of these aspects throughout this interview. But always focus on getting better. When you have an opportunity to communicate with someone, put yourself out there. I remember the first time I spoke on stage. It was such an exhilarating feeling. All I was doing was communicating on this platform. It was such a different way for me to communicate, which I hadn't done before. So, seek out different ways to communicate with others.

Sharpen your skill set by putting in the reps, and thinking about it as a true skill set. It isn't something that you should take lightly, if you want to get anything in life. Being an effective communicator will significantly help you improve the odds of getting whatever goal you want to achieve in life.

Jacqlyn: I'm beyond grateful for the time you spent with me here. Thank you, Casey.

HAPPINESS HABITAT

When you communicate, you not only transfer energy within yourself, you also transfer energy to everyone you interact with. This means that you have the responsibility to not only show up for yourself, but to show up for everyone you come into contact with. Your energy and communication is conveyed through your words, tone, body language, and thoughts. If you operate from a place of love, you can raise everything and everyone around you. Remember, you get what you give. Communication is the foundation of all human interaction. We are all love, joy, and abundance. Convey this through your communication, and you will receive it in return.

You are gifted with the ability to use words and the brainpower to study language. Language can either be a barrier or a bridge. Communication is a skill that you will continue to develop and improve throughout your life; it is the essence of connection.

EXERCISE 8

Improving your communication skills is an important part of being an effective and confident communicator. If you take the time to reflect on your communication style, and identify areas for improvement, you can become more aware of the way you show up in conversations. Then make positive changes to enhance your communication skills. This exercise will help you track and improve your communication in a structured and deliberate way. Follow the steps outlined in this exercise, and you will be able to identify areas for improvement. Come up with a plan to make changes. And track your progress over time. As you practice and implement the changes you have identified, you will see a gradual improvement in your communication skills.

1. Start by setting aside a few minutes each day to reflect on your communication style. Take some time to think about how you show up in conversations. And what does your

body language, tone, and words convey about you?

2. As you go about your day, pay attention to the conversations you have, and the way you communicate. Take note of any moments when you feel like you could have improved your communication. Jot them down in a journal, or on a piece of paper.

3. At the end of each day, review your notes, and identify any patterns or areas where you can improve. For example, you may notice that you tend to get defensive when someone challenges your beliefs. Or, that you sometimes speak too quickly, and don't give others a chance to respond.

4. For each area you identified, come up with a specific action you can take to improve. For example, if you notice that you get defensive when challenged, you could remind yourself to listen and respond with empathy, instead of going on the attack.

5. Put your plan into action the next day, and continue to track your progress over time. As you practice and implement the changes you've identified, you will see ongoing improvement in your communication skills.

HAPPINESS HABITAT

Here are some tips to improve your internal and external communication:

1. Sit up straight with your shoulders back to convey confidence and openness.

2. Have a smile on your face to show that you are approachable and friendly.

3. Be mindful of the words you use, and the meaning behind them. Choose words that are clear, concise, and accurate.

4. Reflect on your values and beliefs every day to ensure that you are communicating in a way that is true to yourself.

5. Operate from a place of love and kindness. This means you treat others with respect and empathy. And be willing to listen and understand their perspective.

6. Know that what you give is what you receive. If you communicate with kindness and understanding, you are

much more likely to receive the same in return.

7. Raise the vibration of your environment by being conscious of the energy you bring into a conversation. Use positive body language, tone, and words to create an engaging and productive atmosphere.

Chapter 8
ENHANCE YOUR BRAINWAVES

"Whatever the mind can conceive and believe, it can achieve."
— *Napoleon Hill*

We've all experienced an "A-ha!" Moment, a flow state, or a state of pure creativity. The key to having more of these experiences is to understand the connections that happen within our brain. At the root of all our thoughts, emotions, and behaviors is the communication between neurons. Brainwaves are produced by synchronized electrical pulses from masses of neurons communicating with each other. Imagine a rippling wave through the crowd of a sports arena – the synchronized electrical activity is what can be defined of as a brainwave.

Neuroscientists have been studying brainwaves using EEG (electroencephalography) for nearly a century. In my own research, I too have focused on studying brainwaves, and have even undergone a week-long training with

Biocybernaut, a pioneer in neurofeedback training, to enhance my own brainwaves. Before I get into that profound experience, I am going to break down the main brainwaves we operate in, as a foundation for understanding the communication within our brains.

Our brainwaves are measured by their amplitudes and frequencies. Here is a list of the five most commonly described brainwaves, from fastest activity to slowest:

Gamma:

- Frequency: 32 – 100 Hz.
- Associated state: Heightened perception, learning, problem-solving tasks.

Gamma brainwaves are the fastest brainwaves measured by EEG. They are linked to heightened perception, peak mental states, and increased cognitive function. Experienced meditators, such as monks, often exhibit higher levels of Gamma brainwaves during deep meditation, or advanced concentration techniques, which indicates their enhanced focus and awareness. However, Gamma brainwaves are not exclusive to meditators, and can also be present in individuals during complex cognitive tasks, problem-solving, or learning. The presence of Gamma brainwaves is generally associated with improved focus, mental performance, and information processing.

Beta:

- Frequency: 13 – 32 Hz.
- Associated state: Awake, alert consciousness, thinking, excitement.

Beta brainwaves are most commonly associated with an alert and focused state of mind. They are prevalent during daily activities that require critical thinking, decision-making, or active conversation. They play a crucial role in our day-to-day functioning by enabling us to process information, solve problems, and engage effectively with our environment. Maintaining a healthy balance between Beta and other brainwave states is essential for overall cognitive function and mental well-being.

Alpha:
- Frequency: 8 – 13 Hz.
- Associated state: Physically and mentally relaxed.

Alpha brainwaves are associated with a relaxed and calm state of mind, typically experienced when the eyes are closed and the mind is at ease. They are often observed during activities like yoga, light meditation, and during the transition between wakefulness and sleep. Alpha promotes a state of relaxed focus that facilitates creative thinking, and access to the subconscious mind. The Alpha state is particularly helpful for enhancing mental well-being, learning, and emotional intelligence, contributing to a more balanced and fulfilling life experience. The Alpha state can feel like a superpower because it enhances various aspects of the human experience, and even overall health.

Theta:
- Frequency: 4 – 8 Hz.
- Associated state: Creativity, insight, deep states, dreams, deep meditation, reduced consciousness.

Theta brainwaves are observed during deep relaxation, right before falling asleep, during deep meditation, or while daydreaming. These brainwaves, slower than both Alpha and Beta, are related to enhanced intuition, creativity, and the exploration of the subconscious mind. The Theta state is unique as it lies between wakefulness and sleep, allowing for distinct mental experiences, vivid visualizations, and insights that may not be accessible during more alert states of consciousness.

Delta:

- Frequency: 0.5 – 4 Hz.
- Associated state: Deep (dreamless) sleep, loss of bodily awareness, repair.

Delta are the slowest brainwaves. They are most prominent during deep, dreamless sleep, and are essential for the restorative functions of the body and mind. Delta waves are associated with the release of healing hormones, regeneration of cells, and strengthening of the immune system. This is why it's so important to get a good night's sleep to experience the benefits of the Delta state.

The brainwave state we operate in most often is Beta, as this is where we engage in active conversation and critical thinking. When we are in a state of flow, we are in Alpha. Our brainwaves change in relation to our feelings and actions. When we are feeling sluggish and tired, our brainwaves are slower. When we are wired and hyper-alert, we experience faster brainwaves. Focusing our brainwaves can be done through neurofeedback training. There are both technology-based and non-technology-based practices that can help fine-tune our ability to access and remain in a certain brainwave state for a desired result. For example, meditation can help us deepen our ability to focus and control our attention. In this chapter though, I will focus on Alpha brainwaves, as this is where a lot of problem-solving can occur.

"Alpha brainwaves are dominant during quietly flowing thoughts, and in some meditative states. Alpha is 'the power of now' being here, in the present. Alpha is the resting state for the brain. Alpha waves aid overall mental coordination, calmness, alertness, mind/body integration and learning." (Brain Work Neurotherapy).

Dr. Jim Hardt has created a system called Biocybernaut to provide a feedback mechanism for the brain. Dr. Hardt is a pioneer in neurofeedback training, helping people tune into Zen-like states in days, instead of decades. I had the privilege of participating in Dr. Hardt's Deluxe Premium Double Alpha One Training in 2019. The goal of the training was to improve my Alpha brainwaves. Electrodes were attached to different areas of my head to measure my brainwaves, and display them on a monitor and a speaker. This allowed me to see and hear my brainwaves in real-time, and my brain adapted accordingly. Each region of my brain made a different noise when Alpha was activated, creating a symphony of sounds. As my Alpha brainwaves became stronger, the sound grew louder. I went through a series of exercises to train my brain. As a result, I was able to increase my creativity, IQ, EQ, peak performance, joy, reverse brain aging; and relieve stress and anxiety, among other benefits. Some of the exercises we did in the training included practicing forgiveness, which can help us access higher states of Alpha. Taking care of our minds, and understanding how we operate, can help us maximize our potential.

During my training with Dr. Jim Hardt I got to dive deep with him on the understanding of brainwaves. Here is a segment from our conversation:

> **Dr. Hardt**: Let's think of different brainwaves as the gears of a car, a manual transmission car. Delta is like first gear. Theta: second gear. Alpha: third gear. Beta: fourth gear. And Gamma is like fifth gear. So, we have a five-speed car. But most people live their lives driving only in first gear or fifth gear. If you drove your car this way you'd be in Delta and Theta. And if you drove your car this way, you'd have low gas mileage and high repair bills. Shifting from first to fifth, and from fifth back to first. Unfortunately, so many people run their brain that way. They are either asleep, and they got there by taking an Ambien, or some type of sleeping pill. Then, when

the alarm goes off, they wake up really tired. They down some coffee. Put themselves into high-frequency Beta. And they are pull-tail boogie jamin' stressed all day long. At night, they shut themselves down again, and they don't spend much time in second, third or fourth gear. So, equivalent to low gas milage and high repair bills is low productivity, low creativity, and high medical costs. Many people say that stress is the basis for 80% of most diseases, and Beta is high stress.

In other words, when Alpha is up, stress and anxiety go down. When Beta is up, stress and anxiety go up. This is not a state you want to spend *all* your time in. Still, it is a state you want to have access to. Beta is good for routine performance and non-interesting tasks. But Alpha is where you can access peak performance and creativity. Alpha is highest naturally in an untrained state when you are in a state of mental arousal. If you are in high stress, you need to relax to access Alpha. Also, if you are depressed or tired, you need to activate and access Alpha.

Another way to enhance Alpha, as shared by Dr. Hardt, is to simply close your eyes. Even if your mind is racing, or if you're in high stress, closing your eyes will enhance Alpha. I practiced this frequently when I was in Dr. Hardt's Biocybernaut Deluxe Premium Double Alpha One training.

> **Dr. Hardt**: You also want to pay attention to your breathing. If you slow down and deepen your breathing, even if a little bit, this will oxygenate your blood more, and blow off more carbon dioxide. When carbon dioxide is absorbed in the blood it forms something called carbonic acid. When you blow that off, the PH of the blood shifts away from acid toward alkaline. This triggers the blood vessels to dilate. Now you have more blood flowing, which the brain loves. The blood has more oxygen in it, which the

brain really loves. And both of these things will contribute to higher Alpha.

When you close your eyes and slow your breathing, you want to avoid visualizations, as this can lower your Alpha. According to Dr. Hardt, only about 5% of the population experiences an increase in Alpha when visualizing, such as meditation teachers. It's okay to have a quick visualization; but then let go of it, and focus on the feeling and intention behind it.

Dr. Hardt shared a story with me about this one time he had a trainee who, whenever she needed to use the bathroom, would first grab her purse. When she returned, she smelled of cigarette smoke. When she went back in the chamber, her Alpha was at 1/10th of where it was before. This was because nicotine quickly enters the blood and constricts blood vessels, depriving the brain of blood and oxygen, which leads to reduced Alpha. Caffeine is also a vasoconstrictor, and it replaces Alpha with Beta, resulting in a busy mind. If someone is in, for example, a secretarial role, and has a lot of noncreative mundane tasks they need to perform quickly, then caffeine can help with that.

Alcohol also reduces Alpha, as it is a brain poison that can kill brain cells; and, if you have a cut, it can enhance infecting agents. Dr. Hardt also mentioned the concept of happy hour, which he believes should be called "happy 45-minute hour" because alcohol can relax tense muscles and raise Alpha for brief periods of time. However, after 45 minutes, the central nervous system suppressing the effects of Alpha kick in, and you may even experience a hangover the next morning. For these reasons, it's best to avoid alcohol, nicotine, and caffeine.

Improving and accessing our Alpha brainwave can be achieved through meditation. Mediation allows us to "be". It allows us to access that state of mental arousal, clear our mind, and let thoughts pass through without interference.

HAPPINESS HABITAT

"One of the most interesting studies in the last few years, carried out at Yale University, found that mindfulness meditation decreases activity in the DMN (default mode network) the brain network responsible for mind-wandering and self-referential thoughts – a.k.a., 'monkey mind'", (Forbes). Consistency is key when it comes to meditation. Meditating for even just two minutes every day is much more impactful than meditating for one hour once a week. The power of consistency can be understood through a simple mathematical analogy: Consistent daily practice has a cumulative effect, similar to how 2 x 2 = 4. In contrast, doing something once a week with gaps in between, yields no cumulative effect. In sum, consistency is key when it comes to the benefits of meditation. And the more consistent you are, the greater the impact. To expand and take care of your brain, meditation can play a vital role in the overall health of your mind, body, and spirit. Meditation doesn't have to be a form of stillness. It can be any activity that brings you a sense of peace, such as calm yoga, painting, writing, or anything creative that resonates with you.

To realize our full ability, it's important to understand our brainwaves. and how to access them effectively. This includes not only our awake state, but also our sleeping state. In the Delta state, our brainwaves can be enhanced and repaired. Delta brainwaves are the slowest of the brainwave frequencies and are typically associated with deep, dreamless sleep. Delta brainwaves are important for a number of reasons, including regulating the body's natural sleep-wake cycle and helping to repair and heal the body during sleep. Delta brainwaves are also associated with increased levels of human growth hormone, which is important for tissue repair and muscle growth. Delta brainwaves play a crucial role in maintaining overall physical and emotional well-being. To maximize Delta, it's important to create a conducive environment for sleep. This involves reducing blue light exposure before bedtime. Also eliminating

LED light from the bedroom, as it can disrupt your sleep patterns. By implementing these practices, you can improve your state of deep sleep and rejuvenation.

Enjoy the process of discovering how you can enhance your brainwave states and improve your focus, concentration, and overall well-being. With this knowledge, you can optimize your performance, and reach your goals more effectively. Don't let the power of your mind go to waste. Take control of your brain and unlock your true potential.

EXERCISE 9

To improve your Alpha brainwaves, start by observing your own behavior and identifying the activities and emotions that bring you into a state of flow. For the next week, try to view yourself from a third-person perspective, and take note of when you are operating in different "gears", as Dr. Hardt described. Are you ever stuck in first gear or fifth gear?

After evaluating your habits and behaviors, implement some of the following tips to improve your Alpha brainwaves:

- Avoid caffeine, alcohol, and nicotine, as these substances will suppress Alpha activity.

- Simply close your eyes and slow down your breathing. Avoiding visualizations when doing so will also increase Alpha.

- Reduce your exposure to blue light, particularly in the evening, as this can disrupt your sleep and decrease Alpha production. Blue light can suppress the production of melatonin, a hormone that helps regulate the sleep-wake cycle, and is important for maintaining overall health and well-being.

- Practice deep breathing exercises. This will increase Alpha activity and promote relaxation.

- Incorporate mindfulness into your daily routine. This will help quiet the "monkey mind" and improve your ability to focus.
- Spend time in nature. This will promote relaxation and increase Alpha activity.
- Engage in activities that you enjoy, and that bring you a sense of peace and fulfillment. This could be painting, journaling, meditating, a nature walk, calling your mom, or whatever feels most joyful to you.

AFTERWORD

Happiness happens when we are inspired. When we are grateful for the present moment, we are happy. When we allow the interference of mostly ego-based emotions such as fear, doubt, anxiety, anger, being offended, or any of the negative feelings we have, we corrupt that connection. Your reactions when operating from these states of consciousness will cause your direction to deviate from what you want; which is happiness.

We all can become inspired. We all have the opportunity to operate at a higher vibration. I hope this book has cleared any interference to function at your true potential. David Meltzer has taught me this powerful lesson, which is the understanding for clearing any mental obstacles that stand in the way of experiencing joy. Optimizing your Opportunity Zone in all aspects of life will build the foundation for your Happiness Habitat.

When you operate from a place of happiness, your lens is clear: To seeing opportunities, to the awareness of yourself, and those around you. And most importantly, how you experience the world. Your mindset dictates your perception, which dictates your reality. It's time to feed your consciousness with the right *nutrients* to maximize your opportunity. A simple way to expand your perspective, and create a more abundant mindset, is by simply changing your perspective. As the famous motivational speaker, Wayne Dyer, said: "Change the way you look at things, and the things you look at change." When you optimize your environment in your inner-world and your outer-world, you will be that much more inspired and effective.

If you follow the blueprint in this book you'll be able to create your dynamic zone for optimization and joy. Just purely by now having read *Happiness Habitat* you've already expanded. You can now operate with this new data, and reflect on the experiential knowledge you have gained. You already have exactly what you need to live your most

HAPPINESS HABITAT

abundant life. Now, go create your Happiness Habitat!

—Jacqlyn Burnett

ACKNOWLEDGMENTS

I am deeply grateful to have the opportunity to write this book and share my journey, lessons, and insights with you. The realization of this project would not have been possible without the support, guidance, and encouragement from many amazing individuals.

First and foremost, my sincere appreciation goes out to Cliff Carle, my editor and writing coach. Cliff, your invaluable expertise, dedication, and patience throughout this journey have been instrumental in shaping this book. You've been more than an editor; you've been a mentor and a friend, and for that, I am profoundly grateful.

I would like to extend my profound gratitude to my parents, Mark and Beverly Burnett, and my younger brother, Alex. You are the bedrock of *Happiness Habitat*. Your constant unconditional love, understanding, and support throughout my life have always inspired me.

Next, I extend heartfelt thanks to my loving partner, Casey Adams. Casey, your unwavering belief in me and my vision has been a source of strength and inspiration.

I am immensely grateful to David Meltzer, my mentor and cousin, whose wisdom and guidance have not only shaped this book, but have significantly influenced my life's trajectory.

My profound appreciation extends to my wonderful friends, who have been my sounding boards, cheerleaders, and counselors throughout this journey.

To everyone I've had the honor of collaborating with, in numerous organizations and projects, thank you for the experiences and opportunities that have become pivotal points in my journey.

HAPPINESS HABITAT

And last but not least, to you, the reader – thank you. It is for you that this book exists. May it guide you as you navigate your path and inspire you to build your own Happiness Habitat.

Unconditionally,
Jacqlyn Burnett

REFERENCES

Quantum Physics:
https://www.equilibrium-e3.com/images/PDF/The%20Research%20of%20Candace%20Pert.pdf
https://johnamaral.com/faq/

Organizing Your Environment:
https://www.ncbi.nlm.nih.gov/pubmed/21228167

What You Consume, Consumes You:
https://health.usnews.com/wellness/food/articles/2017-11-29/the-trouble-with-lectins

The Plant Paradox by Dr. David Gundry:
https://www.diagnosisdiet.com/full-article/grains-beans-nuts-seeds

Communication:
https://www.nytimes.com/2006/09/24/books/chapters/0924-1st-peas.html

Brainwaves:

https://choosemuse.com/blog/a-deep-dive-into-brainwaves-brainwave-frequencies-explained-2/

https://brainworksneurotherapy.com/what-are-brainwaves

https://www.biocybernaut.com

https://www.forbes.com/sites/alicegwalton/2015/02/09/7-ways-meditation-can-actually-change-the-brain/#428f795a1465

CONTRIBUTORS

Dr. George Pratt
https://www.drgeorgepratt.com
https://www.instagram.com/drgeorgepratt

Charlie Rocket
https://charlierocket.com
https://www.instagram.com/charlie

Dr. Carolyn Daitch
https://carolyndaitchphd.com
https://www.instagram.com/dr.carolyn.daitch

Marie Kondo Team
https://konmari.com
https://www.instagram.com/mariekondo

MaryRuth Ghiyam
https://www.maryruthorganics.com
https://www.instagram.com/maryruthorganics

David Meltzer
https://dmeltzer.com
https://www.instagram.com/davidmeltzer

HAPPINESS HABITAT

Casey Adams
https://www.caseyadams.com
https://www.instagram.com/casey

Dr. James Hardt
https://www.biocybernaut.com
https://www.instagram.com/biocybernaut